Contents

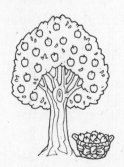

Monroe

Theme: Thanksgiving: Then and Now

Theme: At the Fire Station

Theme: Looking at Leaves

Theme: Monster Mania

Contents
Sensational Seasons: Fall, SV 9781419033957

Introduction

Preschool curriculum and instruction have been dramatically affected by the federal legislation that demands that schools *Put Reading First* and *No Child Is Left Behind* in achieving reading and math skills. Currently, the most important instructional focus in preschool classrooms is literacy development—providing environments in which young children can explore words, language, books, and print through developmentally appropriate literacy events.

In a literacy-rich classroom, children are surrounded with print, and their days are filled with activities that invite them to interact with print. Children are encouraged to "pretend" or attempt to read and write. Their attempts at reading and writing emergently are honored and valued as children move through the stages of development to become conventional readers and writers. So, the preschool teacher's role has changed from one of getting children "ready" to read to one of getting children reading and writing.

Activities Can Enrich Preschoolers' Literacy Experience

First Page of Each Unit Provides:

- Book List
- Teacher Information (Facts)

Second Page of Each Unit Provides:

- Illustrated Bulletin Board
- Materials List
- Teacher Preparation
- Student Directions

Third and Fourth Pages Provide Circle Time Lessons That Include:

- Standard
- Language Arts, Math, and/or Science Skills
- Song or Poem

Fifth Page of Each Unit Provides:

- Standard
- Writing Activity
- Simple Snack Idea

Sixth and Seventh Pages Provide Center Ideas That Include:

- Standard
- Math Center Activity
- Language Center Activity
- Other Center Activities (Art, Science, Sensory)

Remaining Pages of Each Unit Provide:

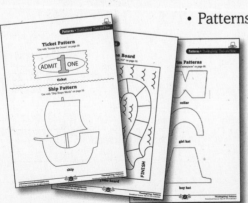

- Patterns and/or Activity Masters

Introduction
Sensational Seasons: Fall, SV 9781419033957

Standards

The following are preschool standards included with the activities and lessons in this book. Use these standards to guide further practice and to measure progress.

Language Arts	Page(s)
Recognizes and names letters of the alphabet	11, 12, 13, 41
Shows awareness that different words begin with the same sound	11, 68, 78
Understands that letters make sounds	11, 31, 49
Uses scribbles, approximations of letters, or known letters to represent written language	13, 86
Matches partner letters	14, 23, 69, 87
Identifies letters in own name	15
Identifies labels in the environment	20
Engages in conversations that develop a thought or idea	20, 86
Begins to distinguish letters in written text	21, 56
Writes to produce numbers	22
Experiments with new vocabulary	22
Stays with or repeats a task	24, 42
Begins to distinguish words in sentences	20, 29, 67
Responds to simple questions about stories	30
Communicates information with others	30, 39
Makes illustrations to match sentences	31, 58, 68
Predicts what will happen next using pictures and content for guides	32, 38, 47
Begins to identify onsets and rimes	38
Listens with understanding and responds to directions	39, 40
Understands that different texts such as letters, notes, or lists are used for different purposes	40, 57
Recognizes and names rhyming words	47, 48, 56, 85
Writes to produce letters of the alphabet	49
Retells a story in sequence using illustrations	50
Demonstrates some ability to hear separate syllables in words	57
Begins to recognize high-frequency words	59
Relates prior knowledge to new information	66
Understands that reading progresses from left to right	66, 75, 84
Begins to understand and name opposites	67
Demonstrates an understanding of letters and words	75

Language Arts	Page(s)
Participates in songs that emphasize sounds and rhymes	76
Uses drawing and writing skills to convey meaning and information	77
Retells information from a story	84
Follows two-step requests that are sequential but not related	84
Acts out plays, stories, or songs	88

Math	Page(s)
Sorts objects by one or two attributes	12
Begins to compare groups and recognize more than, less than, and equal to relationships	14, 21, 29
Counts objects using one-to-one correspondence	23, 32, 41
Solves simple mathematical problems	38
Names common shapes	48
Uses concepts that include number recognition and counting	50, 59, 69
Represents data using concrete objects, pictures, and graphs	56, 76, 77
Uses measuring implements	58
Demonstrates a beginning understanding of measurement	60, 78
Recognizes and names numbers	66
Uses positional terms such as in, on, over, or under	85
Describes and extends simple patterns	87

Science	Page(s)
Examines organisms by paying attention to detail	33, 79
Uses senses to observe and explore materials	51, 70
Demonstrates a willingness to take risks by choosing to participate in a variety of experiences	88

Art	Page(s)
Explores a variety of techniques to create original work	15, 24, 33, 42, 60, 70
Explores a variety of tools to create original work	51
Explores a variety of materials to create original work	79

www.harcourtschoolsupply.com
© Harcourt Achieve Inc. All rights reserved.

Standards
Sensational Seasons: Fall, SV 9781419033957

Rhyming Picture Cards

The following cards may be used as a center activity, allowing children to match rhyming word cards, sort the cards into categories, or make up silly rhymes using the rhyming word pairs.

can

fan

cat

rat

jet

net

pig

wig

Rhyming Picture Cards

mop

top

gum

drum

sail

nail

bee

tree

Rhyming Picture Cards
Sensational Seasons: Fall, SV 9781419033957

Rhyming Picture Cards

boat

coat

dime

time

jar

car

hair

chair

Rhyming Picture Cards
Sensational Seasons: Fall, SV 9781419033957

A Is for Alphabet

Books to Read

Alphabet Adventure by Audrey Wood (Blue Sky Press)

Alphabet Under Construction by Denise Fleming (Henry Holt & Co.)

Arf! Beg! Catch!: Dogs from A to Z by Henry Horenstein (Scholastic)

Chicka Chicka Boom Boom by Bill Martin, Jr. (Aladdin Picture Books)

Dr. Seuss's ABC by Dr. Seuss (Random House Books for Young Readers)

G Is for Goat by Patricia Polacco (Puffin)

Miss Spider's ABC by David Kirk (Scholastic)

The Alphabet Tree by Leo Lionni (Dragonfly)

26 Letters and 99 Cents by Tana Hoban (Greenwillow)

Alphabet Facts

The English alphabet consists of 26 letters that include consonants and vowels. Learning about the letters of the alphabet and the sounds that they make is achieved through phonological awareness. Phonological awareness is the understanding that sentences are made of words, words are made of syllables, and syllables are made of sounds, or phonemes. Phonemic awareness is a part of phonological awareness in that it refers to smaller sound units, or phonemes. Both phonological and phonemic awareness involve oral tasks, whereas phonics activities involve print. Phonics refers to letter-sound correspondences. A strong phonological awareness gives young children a foundation on which to build reading and spelling skills.

Sensational Seasons: Fall, SV 9781419033957

Letter Creatures

Materials

- any color of craft paper
- border
- various colors of construction paper
- a generous supply of craft items such as sequins, wiggly eyes, yarn, buttons, and glitter
- crayons or markers
- scrap paper
- scissors
- glue
- stapler

Directions

Teacher Preparation: Draw on construction paper a large copy of the first letter of each child's name. Cover the bulletin board with craft paper. Add a border and the caption.

1. Invite children to use the craft items to create a letter creature by adding features to the letter.

2. Have children write or dictate labels for their creatures, giving them alliterative names such as *Alex the Astronaut, Billy the Busy Boy,* or *Cathy the Cat.*

3. Staple the letter creatures to the bulletin board in a pleasing arrangement.

Finger Puppet Fun

Language Arts Standard: *Recognizes and names letters of the alphabet*

- Make a set of cards that have two letters on each card. Write the same two letters on some cards and two different letters on others.

- Duplicate two finger puppets (p. 16) for each child to cut out. Younger children may need help with cutting.

- Have children draw a happy face on one puppet and a sad face on the other.

- Help them to tape the finger puppets so they fit on their fingers.

- Invite children to put one finger puppet on each hand.

- Hold up one letter card and have children wiggle the happy face puppet if the letters are the same or the sad face if the letters are different.

- Challenge children to name the letters on the cards.

Going On a Letter Hunt

Language Arts Standard: *Shows awareness that different words begin with the same sound*

- Write three target letters across the top of a chart.

- Make picture cards of objects whose names begin with the sounds of the target letters. Hide the cards around the room. Hide a card for each child.

- Invite children to find a card and then sit in a circle around the chart.

- Have children use double-sided tape to stick their card on the chart below the letter that has the same beginning sound as the object on their card.

Looking at Letters and Words

Language Arts Standard: *Understands that letters make sounds*

- Show children pictures of farm animals such as a cow, a pig, a dog, and a duck.

- Invite children to make the sounds that the animals make as each picture is shown. Emphasize that each animal makes its own sound.

- Have children look at the classroom alphabet picture cards.

- Tell children that letters of the alphabet are like the animals because each letter makes its own sound.

- Challenge children to say the sound of each letter as you point to it.

Sensational Seasons: Fall, SV 9781419033957

Curved or Straight Letters

Math Standard: *Sorts objects by one or two attributes*

• Make labels that have a straight line, a curved line, and both lines on them. Tape each label to a shallow box or lid.

• Make a set of alphabet flashcards using only uppercase letters.

• Lay the cards across the floor or table for children to see.

• Point out that some letters of the alphabet are made with straight lines, some are made with curved lines, and some are made with both.

• Mix up the cards and put them facedown in a stack.

• Invite children to take turns picking the top card from the stack.

• Challenge children to tell if the letter is made with straight lines, curved lines, or both.

• Have children put the letter card in the box with the correct label.

• Encourage children to count how many letter cards are in each box at the end of the activity.

In Tune with Language

Language Arts Standard: *Recognizes and names letters of the alphabet*

• Invite children to play the circle alphabet game. Have them learn the following rhyme.

  A tisket, a tasket,
  A green and yellow basket.
  I wrote a letter to my friend
  And on the way I dropped it.
  I dropped it.
  And on the way I dropped it.

• Provide children with a basket filled with alphabet letter cards.

• Have children take turns dropping an alphabet letter card behind a child each time the game is played.

• Challenge the receiver to pick up the card and name the letter before the child with the basket returns to that spot.

Let's Write: *A Is for Apple*

Language Arts Standard: *Uses scribbles, approximations of letters, or known letters to represent written language*

• Read an alphabet book such as *G Is for Goat* by Patricia Polacco. Have children notice that the book goes through the alphabet from *A* to *Z*.

• Make a list of the letters from *A* to *Z* on a chart.

• Invite children to name foods whose names begin with each letter of the alphabet. For the letter *K*, children may use the word *kiwi*. For the letter *V*, children may use the word *vegetables*. If they cannot think of a food, leave the letter blank. By leaving some letters blank, children will become aware that some letters of the alphabet are not used as frequently.

• Write children's responses next to the letters on the chart.

• Encourage children to choose a food from the list.

• Invite children to draw a picture of the food they chose.

• Have them write the name of the food they chose and underline the letter it begins with. For younger children, you may accept scribble writing or letter approximations.

Alphabet Letter Pretzels

Language Arts Standard: *Recognizes and names letters of the alphabet*

• Have children measure and mix in a bowl two cups of flour, three-fourths to one cup of water, and one tablespoon of sugar.

• Invite children to knead the dough on a floured surface.

• Provide each child with a two-inch ball of dough.

• Have children roll the dough in long ropes and form the first letter of their name.

• Invite children to beat one egg in a bowl with a whisk or fork.

• Then have them brush their formed letter with egg and sprinkle it with coarse salt. Bake at 400°F until brown.

• Encourage children to take turns saying the name of their letter before eating it.

Caution: Be aware of children who may have food allergies.

Sensational Seasons: Fall, SV 9781419033957

Math Center

Math Standard:
Begins to compare groups and recognize more than, less than, and equal to relationships

Comparing Names

- Draw a grid on a six-inch by twenty-inch sheet of craft paper. Make two rows and ten columns. Laminate it for durability.

- Make a name card on a sentence strip for each child.

- Provide children with a set of plastic letters. Include duplicates of common letters and vowels.

- Invite partners to find plastic letters that match those in each of their names.

- Have each child spell his or her name by putting a letter in each box on separate rows of the grid.

- Have children count the letters in each of their names.

- Challenge them to tell which name has more letters, fewer letters, or the same number of letters.

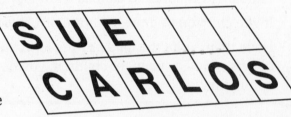

Language Center

Language Arts Standard:
Matches partner letters

Letter Puzzles

- Enlarge and duplicate the letter cards (p. 16 and p. 17).

- Cut them out and glue them to index cards. Then laminate them.

- Cut each card in half to make simple puzzles.

- Invite children to put the puzzles together by matching partner letters. For younger children, select puzzles for four or five target letters rather than the entire alphabet.

- Encourage children to look at the classroom alphabet chart for guidance.

Art Center

Art Standard:
Explores a variety of techniques to create original work

Gluey, Glittery Letters

- Make uppercase letter cards on half sheets of construction paper. Each letter should be about four inches tall.
- Provide each child with a piece of waxed paper cut to fit the letter cards.
- Have children lay the waxed paper on top of a letter card of their choice, such as the first letter in their name.
- Invite children to use glue to copy the letter onto the waxed paper. Encourage them to make thick lines of glue and to connect all of the "strokes."
- Have children sprinkle glitter on the glue. Allow the glue to dry.
- Help children peel the waxed paper off of their letter.
- Hang the letters around the classroom with a piece of yarn or string.

Sensory Center

Language Arts Standard:
Identifies letters in own name

Digging for Letters

- Bury a set of magnetic letters and a small plastic shovel in the sand table.
- Place a metal cookie sheet in or near the sand table.
- Write children's names on sentence strips.
- Invite children to find the letters in their name by looking for the magnetic letters in the sand.
- Have children use the magnetic letters to spell their name on the cookie sheet.

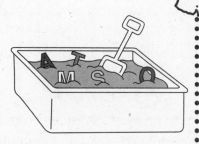

Finger Puppet Patterns
Use with "Finger Puppet Fun" on page 11.

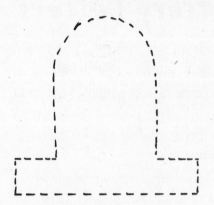 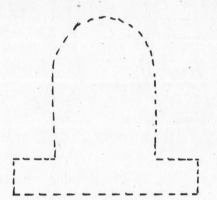

finger puppet   **finger puppet**

Alphabet Letter Cards
Use with "Letter Puzzles" on page 14.

A a	B b	C c
D d	E e	F f
G g	H h	I i
J j	K k	L l

Sensational Seasons: Fall, SV 9781419033957

More Alphabet Letter Cards

Use with "Letter Puzzles" on page 14.

M m	N n	O o
P p	Q q	R r
S s	T t	U u
V v	W w	X x
Y y	Z z	

Alphabet: Letter Cards
Sensational Seasons: Fall, SV 9781419033957

An Apple a Day

Books to Read

Apples by Gail Gibbons (Holiday House)

Apples, Apples, Apples by Nancy Elizabeth Wallace (Winslow Press)

How Do Apples Grow? by Betsy Maestro and Giulio Maestro (HarperTrophy)

I Am an Apple by Jean Marzollo (Scholastic)

Little Mouse and the Big Red Apple by A. H. Benjamin (Tiger Tales)

Ten Apples Up on Top! by Theo LeSieg (Random House Books for Young Readers)

Ten Red Apples by Pat Hutchins (Greenwillow)

The Seasons of Arnold's Apple Tree by Gail Gibbons (Harcourt, Inc.)

Up, Up, Up! It's Apple Picking Time by Jody Fickes Shapiro (Holiday House)

Apple Facts

There are over 2,500 different kinds of apples in the United States. Apples are grown commercially in 36 states, with the state of Washington growing the most. Apples come in red, yellow, and green or a combination of colors. An apple tree takes from 4 to 5 years to produce its first fruit. Apples are a member of the rose family. Most apple blossoms are pink when they open and gradually fade to white. Apples have 5 seed pockets called carpals. The number of seeds varies according to the type of apple. The freshest apples can float because 25 percent of their volume is air. One tree can produce enough apples to fill 20 boxes that weigh nearly 42 pounds each.

Sensational Seasons: Fall, SV 9781419033957

Apples by the Bushel

Materials

- blue and brown craft paper
- border
- green and brown construction paper
- small paper plates
- red tempera paint
- paintbrushes
- scissors
- glue
- tape
- stapler

Directions

Teacher Preparation: Cover the board with blue craft paper. Add a border and the caption. Cut 12 strips from brown craft paper that are 2 feet long and 3 inches wide. Weave the strips together to form a woven mat. Use scissors to round the corners of the mat so that it resembles a bushel basket. Staple the paper basket to the center of the bulletin board. Add an additional strip across the top for the rim of the basket.

1. Paint the bottom side of the paper plate red. Allow it to dry.

2. Draw and cut out a stem from brown construction paper. Younger children may need help drawing the stem.

3. Draw and cut out a leaf from green construction paper. Accept any shape that children draw.

4. Glue the stem and leaf to the red paper plate to make the apple.

5. Staple the apples to the bulletin board so that they are piled in the bushel basket. Staple any extra apples on each side of the basket in a pleasing arrangement.

Apple Parts

Language Arts Standard: *Identifies labels in the environment*

- Show children an apple that has a stem. Ask them to describe how the apple looks.
- Provide children with crayons and drawing paper. Tell them that they are going to draw the parts of the apple.
- Tell them that the stem is what holds the apple on the tree and the skin is the outside covering of the apple. Demonstrate how to draw an apple with a stem and how to color the skin. Label the parts of the apple.
- Have children draw the apple.
- Cut the apple in half to show the inside parts. Demonstrate how to draw the core, seeds, and meat of the apple.
- Have children draw the inside of the apple.
- Challenge children to identify the labels of the parts of the apples.

The Star in the Apple

Language Arts Standard: *Engages in conversations that develop a thought or idea*

- Tell children the following riddle:

  Deep in the woods there is a little house that is round, has a window on the outside, a little chimney on top, and a star inside.

- Have children guess and then show them the apple with light reflected on it to make a window and a stem "chimney." Then slice the apple in half horizontally. Show children the star inside.
- Have children guess how many seeds are in the apple. Then have them count the seeds as they are removed from the core. Tell them that all apples have five seed pockets.

Looking at Letters and Words

Language Arts Standard: *Begins to distinguish words in sentences*

- Read *The Seasons of Arnold's Apple Tree* by Gail Gibbons. Discuss with children the four seasons.
- Write the word *apple* on the board. Have children find the word in the title of the book.
- On a large sheet of craft paper, draw four trees that are about two feet high and have bare branches. Above each tree, write the name of one of the four seasons. Hang the craft paper on the wall at a child's eye level.
- Invite one child at a time to draw details on a tree according to the name of the season written above it. Allow all children to have a turn.
- Encourage children to draw snow and a snowman with chalk for the tree in winter.

An Apple Graph

Math Standard: *Begins to compare groups and recognize more than, less than, and equal to relationships*

- Prepare a graph with three columns on a large sheet of craft paper. At the top of each column, draw a picture of a red apple, a green apple, and a yellow apple. Hang the graph on the wall.

- Take an individual photo of each child or duplicate a copy of a photo that can be used on the graph. Cut the photos to fit the size of the cells on the graph and stick double-sided tape on the back of each one.

- Show children a red apple, a green apple, and a yellow apple. Invite them to describe each apple and compare them.

- Cut the apples into bite sizes. Provide children with a paper plate and a piece of each apple. Have children eat one piece at a time and describe how it tastes as they chew it slowly.

- Invite children to stick their picture on the graph in the column below their favorite kind of apple.

- Have children look at the completed graph and tell which apple has the most, the least, or the same number of votes.

In Tune with Language

Language Arts Standard: *Begins to distinguish letters in written text*

- Write the rhyme "Way Up High in the Apple Tree" on a chart. Laminate the chart.

**Way up high in the apple tree,
Two little apples smiled at me.
I shook that tree as hard as I could.
Down came the apples.
Ummmm, they were good!**

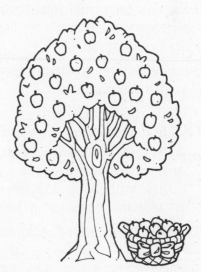

- Explain that *apple* begins with the letter *a*. Show children how to write a lowercase *a*.

- Invite children to use a washable marker to find and circle each letter *a* in the rhyme.

- When each letter *a* has been circled, have children count how many times the letter *a* appears in the rhyme.

Let's Write: Apple Word Books

Language Arts Standard: *Writes to produce numbers*

- Enlarge the apple pattern (p. 25) for use as a template. Trace the apple shape on red construction paper to make a cover and on white paper for book pages. Cut out from three to five pages for each child ahead of time. Have children cut out the apple shape for the cover. Staple the cover and pages together to make an apple book. Add a stem and leaf to the cover if desired.

- Have children draw one apple on the first page of the book. Write *1 apple* on the board as a model. Invite children to write *1 apple* on the page below their drawing. Encourage younger children to use scribble writing to practice pre-writing skills.

- According to the abilities of children, repeat the procedure on other pages of the book with two apples, three apples, and so on.

Crunchy Apples and Yogurt

Language Arts Standard: *Experiments with new vocabulary*

- Core and cut apples into slices.

- Provide each child with a paper plate, a few slices of apples, and a small paper cup of flavored yogurt.

- Invite children to dip the apple slices into the yogurt and eat them.

- While children are eating their apple slices, have them describe how the yogurt and apple tastes. Write their descriptive words such as *yummy, sweet, sour,* and *crunchy* on the board. As each word is written, have children count the letters in the word or have them identify the beginning sound of the word.

Caution: Be aware of children who may have food allergies.

Math Center

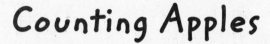

Math Standard:
Counts objects using one-to-one correspondence

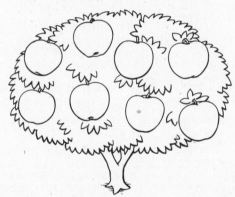

Counting Apples

- Duplicate ten apple trees (p. 26) for use as counting boards and a generous supply of apple counters (p. 25). Color, cut out, and laminate the trees and the counters.

- Write a number from 1 to 10 on each of the counting boards.

- Invite children to place the correct number of apple counters on each board.

- For younger children, have them repeat counting the same target number on each board to practice rote counting.

Language Center

Language Arts Standard:
Matches partner letters

Apple Puzzles

- Duplicate several apples (p. 25) on red construction paper. Cut them out and laminate them.

- Cut each apple in half using a simple puzzle cut.

- Write a target letter on each apple half and write the partner letter on the matching half.

- Invite children to match the apple halves with the partner letters.

- For a phonemic awareness activity, draw or cut out pictures whose names have the same beginning sound as the target letters. Glue the pictures on the matching half of the apples.

Sensational Seasons: Fall, SV 9781419033957

Art Center

Art Standard:
Explores a variety of techniques to create original work

Apple Print Art

- Paint the palm, fingers, and wrist of each child with brown paint. Press them onto white construction paper to make the trunk and branches of an apple tree.

- Drop a few small dots of thinned green paint on the paper among the branches. Have children blow through a clean straw to spread the green paint to resemble the leaves of the tree. Allow the paint to dry.

- Cut an apple in half vertically. Insert a fork securely into the apple as a handle. Pour red paint into a shallow dish.

- Put the picture of the tree on a folded towel, which will act as a pad for the apple print.

- Have children dip the apple into the red paint and make several prints on the branches of the tree.

Sensory Center

Language Arts Standard:
Stays with or repeats a task

Putting Seeds in a Basket

- Make a small apple basket from a paper cup and a pipe cleaner. Punch two holes in the sides of the cup. Cut the pipe cleaner in half and insert each end through the holes of the cup. Twist the ends of the pipe cleaner to form a handle for the apple basket.

- Save real apple seeds or provide a generous supply of black beans for use as "seeds." Place the seeds or beans in a bowl with a pair of tweezers.

- Have children use the tweezers to fill the apple basket with seeds.

Apples: Centers
Sensational Seasons: Fall, SV 9781419033957

Apple Pattern
Use with "Apple Word Books" on page 22 and "Apple Puzzles" on page 23.

apple

Apple Counters
Use with "Counting Apples" on page 23.

Apples: Patterns
Sensational Seasons: Fall, SV 9781419033957

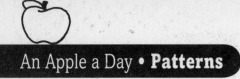
Apple Tree Counting Board

Use with "Counting Apples" on page 23.

tree

Sensational Seasons: Fall, SV 9781419033957

Books to Read

Be Nice to Spiders by Margaret Bloy Graham (HarperCollins)
Diary of a Spider by Doreen Cronin (Joanna Cotler)
Miss Spider's Tea Party by David Kirk (Scholastic)
Spectacular Spiders by Linda Glaser (Millbrook Press)
Spiders by Gail Gibbons (Holiday House)
Spider's Lunch by Joanna Cole (Grosset & Dunlap)
Spiders Spin Webs by Yvonne Winer (Charlesbridge Publishing)
The Itsy Bitsy Spider by Iza Trapani (Charlesbridge Publishing)
The Very Busy Spider by Eric Carle (Scholastic)

Spider Facts

Spiders are arachnids that have eight legs and two major body parts, the cephalothorax (the head and chest) and the abdomen. The eight jointed legs are attached to the cephalothorax, and each leg has a tiny claw at the end that is used for climbing and for manipulating silk. Most spiders have eight eyes. Web building spiders have poor eyesight, while hunting spiders have excellent eyesight for short distances. Spiders have fangs on each side of their mouth that inject poison and paralyze their prey. Next to the fangs are two pedipalps that help cut and crush food. Spiders have silk spinning glands at the tip of their abdomen called spinnerets. Liquid silk comes from the gland in the abdomen and hardens. The silk is used for spinning webs, building traps, protecting eggs, wrapping prey, making safety lines, and ballooning. Baby spiders are called spiderlings. When they hatch, they release silk threads and allow the wind to lift them into the air like a balloon and then land in a new area.

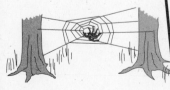

Sensational Seasons: Fall, SV 9781419033957

Our Special Spiders

Materials

- spider pattern (p. 34)
- black craft paper
- border
- brown construction paper
- white chalk
- a fine-tip black marker
- scissors
- glue
- stapler

Directions

Teacher Preparation: Duplicate a spider on brown construction paper for each child. Cut 1-inch by 6-inch strips from the brown paper. For younger children, draw small dots on the spider body to indicate where to glue the legs. Cover the bulletin board with black craft paper and draw a large orb web with white chalk to cover the board. Add a border and the caption.

Read a spider book from the list on page 27 to introduce children to the actual names and functions of the body parts of a spider.

1. Cut out the brown spider body.

2. Accordion fold eight paper strips for the legs.

3. Glue four legs on each side of the large part of the spider. Overlap the strips to fit.

4. Use a black marker to draw eight eyes on the spider.

5. Staple the spiders in a pleasing arrangement on the bulletin board.

All About Spiders

Language Arts Standard: *Begins to distinguish words in sentences*

- Use the spider (p. 34) as a model to draw several large spiders about six inches long. Color, cut out, and laminate them.

- On the back of each, write a spider fact such as the ones below.

  Spiders have eight legs and eight eyes.
  Spiders make webs to catch food.
  Baby spiders are called spiderlings.

- Make a web out of white yarn on the floor and lay the paper spiders on the web. Have children sit around the web.

- Invite children to take turns picking up one spider. Turn it over and read aloud the fact written on the back.

- On the board list key words from each fact such as *legs, eyes, webs,* and *spiderlings.*

- Have children look at the sentences written on the spiders and find the key words.

Sticky Webs

Math Standard: *Begins to compare groups and recognize more than, less than, and equal to relationships*

- Provide each child with 2 paper plates and 12 spider rings. Lima beans can be used if spider rings are not available. You will need 2 large number cubes.

- Invite children to use a black marker to draw lines on both plates to resemble webs. Have them write a number *1* on one plate and a number *2* on the second.

- Roll the first number cube. Have children count the same number of spiders and put them on the web on the first plate.

- Roll the second cube and repeat the procedure on the second plate.

- Challenge children to compare the number of spiders on the first plate to the number on the second plate.

- Have children tell which web has more spiders, which has fewer spiders, or if the webs have the same number of spiders.

- Continue rolling the cubes as long as children show interest.

Nonfiction and Fiction

Language Arts Standard: *Responds to simple questions about stories*

- Show children a nonfiction book about spiders. Explain that a nonfiction book tells true facts about spiders.

- Read the book aloud and discuss with children some of the facts they learned about spiders.

- Explain that a fiction book is a made-up story. Read a fiction storybook about spiders such as *The Very Busy Spider* by Eric Carle or *Be Nice to Spiders* by Margaret Bloy Graham.

- Invite children to compare the nonfiction book about spiders to a fiction storybook about spiders.

- Have children tell if there were any true facts about spiders in the fiction storybook they read.

In Tune with Language

Language Arts Standard: *Communicates information with others*

- Invite children to sing the song "The Itsy Bitsy Spider." Demonstrate the finger actions that can be done with the song and encourage children to do the actions as they sing.

 The itsy bitsy spider
 Went up the waterspout.
 Down came the rain
 And washed the spider out.
 Out came the sun
 And dried up all the rain
 And the itsy bitsy spider
 Went up the spout again.

- Have children tell what they know about a waterspout.

- Challenge them to think of other verses for the song, such as *The great big spider went up the waterspout* or *The little brown spider went up the waterspout.*

Let's Write: Where Is the Spider?

Language Arts Standard: *Makes illustrations to match sentences*

- Have children sing the song "The Itsy Bitsy Spider" on page 30.

- Lead a discussion with them about other places that they might see a spider.

- Model how to write the sentence *I see a spider* _____ .

- Provide children with drawing paper and crayons or markers.

- Have children complete the sentence by writing or dictating words that tell where they might see a spider, such as *I see a spider under the car* or *I see a spider on the table.*

- Invite children to illustrate their sentence.

Scrumptious Spiders

Language Arts Standard: *Understands that letters make sounds*

- Provide each child with a paper plate. Have children use a small tube of colored frosting to draw a spider web on their plate.

- Challenge them to sound spell the word *web*. Write the word *web* on the board for children to see.

- Provide children with two cream filled cookies and eight Chinese noodles.

- Have children lay the cookies side by side in the middle of the web.

- Invite them to stick the eight noodles into the cream part of one cookie with four on each side.

- Have children use the tube of frosting to make eight eyes on the spider.

Caution: Be aware of children who may have food allergies.

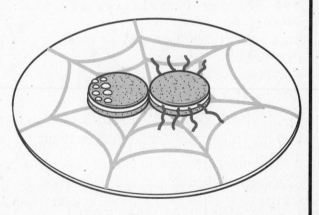

Math Center

Math Standard:
Counts objects using one-to-one correspondence

Spider Web Beanbag Toss

- Draw a large spider web on craft paper, leaving wide spaces between the lines of the web. In random order, write a number from 0 to 3 in each section of the web. Repeat the numbers as often as needed. Tape the paper to the floor. Put a beanbag and 20 plastic spider rings in a bowl near the web.

- Invite children to stand several feet from the "web" and toss the beanbag. Have them name the number on which it lands.

- Have children put the corresponding number of spider rings on their fingers.

- Have children continue taking turns until their fingers are full of rings.

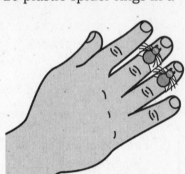

Little Miss Muffet in Order

- Duplicate sequence cards (p. 35) for each child.

- Provide each child with a sheet of construction paper, scissors, crayons, and glue.

- Invite children to sing the song "Little Miss Muffet."

Little Miss Muffet sat on a tuffet,
Eating her curds and whey.
Along came a spider and sat down beside her,
And frightened Miss Muffet away.

- Have children cut out the cards and glue them on the construction paper in the correct sequence. Draw a happy face in the upper left-hand corner of the paper to guide children to start on the left side.

- Invite children to color the pictures on the cards.

Language Center

Language Arts Standard:
Predicts what will happen next using pictures and content for guides

Art Center

Art Standard:
Explores a variety of techniques to create original work

Spider Web Art

- Cut black construction paper to fit the bottom of a shallow box such as a shoe box.
- Put white tempera paint, several marbles, and a spoon in a bowl. Use the spoon to coat all the marbles with paint.
- Invite children to lay the black paper in the bottom of the box.
- Have children pick up the marbles with the spoon and drop them into the box onto the paper.
- Have children put the lid on the box and shake it so the marbles roll around inside to make a "web" design.
- Have children remove the paper and allow it to dry.
- Help children tape a spider ring on the "web."

Science Center

Science Standard:
Examines organisms by paying attention to detail

Take a Good Look

- Discuss with children the two parts of a spider's body, the eight legs, and the multiple eyes (most spiders have eight eyes).
- Display pictures or books that show pictures of spiders or display plastic spiders.
- Invite children to draw a picture of a spider by looking at the plastic spiders or at a picture in a book.

Sensational Seasons: Fall, SV 9781419033957

Spider Pattern

Use with "Our Special Spiders" on page 28 and "All About Spiders" on page 29.

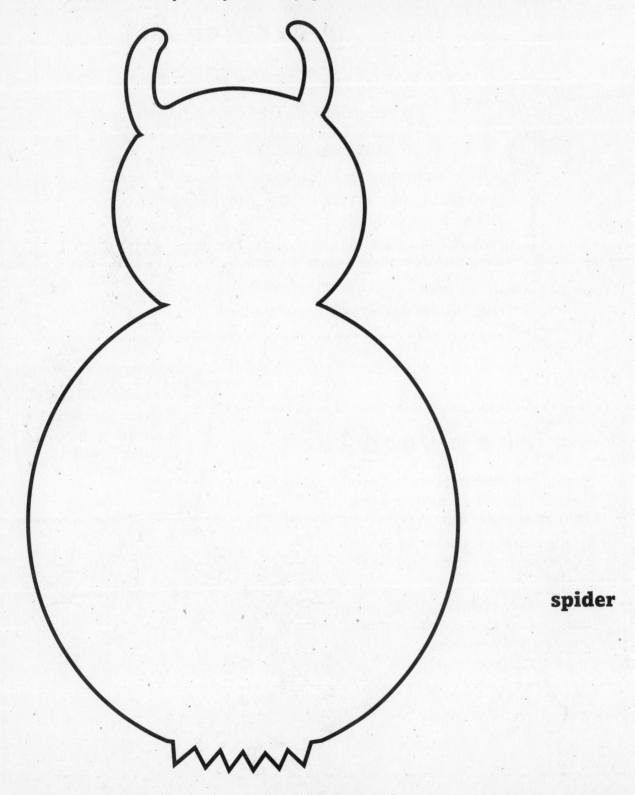

spider

Spiders: Pattern
Sensational Seasons: Fall, SV 9781419033957

Sequence Picture Cards

Use with "Little Miss Muffet in Order" on page 32.

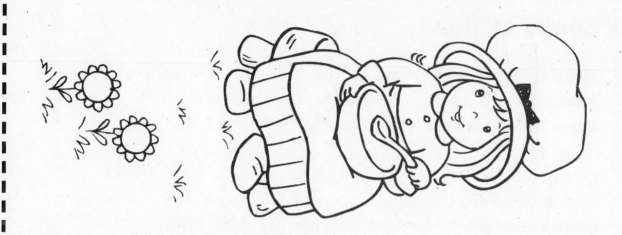

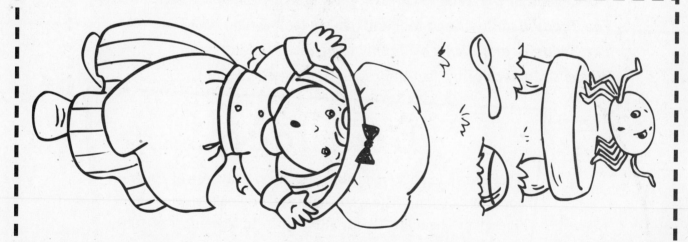

Spiders: Sequence Cards
Sensational Seasons: Fall, SV 9781419033957

Books to Read

Alphabears: An ABC Book by Kathleen Hague (Henry Holt & Co.)

Blueberries for Sal by Robert McCloskey (Puffin Books)

Brown Bear, Brown Bear, What Do You See? by Bill Martin, Jr. (Henry Holt & Co.)

Corduroy by Don Freeman (Puffin Books)

Deep in the Forest by Brinton Turkle (Rebound by Sagebrush)

Goldilocks and the Three Bears by Jan Brett (Putnam Juvenile)

The Legend of the Teddy Bear by Frank Murphy (Sleeping Bear Press)

The Teddy Bear by David McPhail (Henry Holt & Co.)

The Teddy Bear's Picnic by Jimmy Kennedy (Aladdin)

Where's My Teddy? by Jez Alborough (Candlewick Press)

Bear Facts

The cute and cuddly teddy bear has been a favorite of children for over a century. The teddy bear was originally named after President Theodore "Teddy" Roosevelt. In November of 1902, President Roosevelt was on a hunting trip and came upon a bear. The bear was surrounded and helpless. Although President Roosevelt's hunting guide encouraged him to shoot the bear and win a hunting trophy, he refused. News reporters spread the news of his kind act, and a cartoonist drew a cartoon based on the rescue of the bear. A store owner in New York saw the cartoon and decided to make toy bears to sell in his shop. With the permission of President Roosevelt, he called the toys "Teddy's Bear." Today they are known simply as teddy bears.

Sensational Seasons: Fall, SV 9781419033957

Our Cuddly Cubs

Materials

- completed bears from "A Chocolate Teddy Bear" on page 42
- any color of craft paper
- border
- construction paper
- lined writing paper
- glue
- scissors
- stapler

My name is **Fuzzy**.   My name is **Teddy**.   My name is **Brownie**.

Directions

Teacher Preparation:

Cover the bulletin board with craft paper. Add the caption and a border.

1. Tell children about the origination of the teddy bear (p. 36) and that baby bears are called cubs.

2. Invite children to complete the sentence *My bear's name is* _____ . Have them write or dictate a name for their "Chocolate Teddy Bear" on lined writing paper.

3. Have children cut out their bear. Younger children may need help with cutting.

4. Have children glue their bear on construction paper.

5. Have them glue their sentence below their bear painting.

6. Staple the bears on the bulletin board in a pleasing arrangement.

Storybook Bears

Language Arts Standard: *Predicts what will happen next using pictures and content for guides*

- Read a book about storybook bears such as *Blueberries for Sal* by Robert McCloskey, *Where's My Teddy?* by Jez Alborough, or *Goldilocks and the Three Bears* by Jan Brett.
- Have children predict what will happen before reading the end of the story.
- Encourage them to look at the illustrations to help with their predictions.
- Have children retell the story to check for levels of comprehension.

How Many Bears?

Math Standard: *Solves simple mathematical problems*

- Provide each child with a small paper cup full of tiny bear cookies and a napkin to use as a counting board.
- Invite children to count the correct number of bears on their counting board to solve the following word problems. Have them eat the bear cookies when they have solved the problem.

 There were 3 bears in the forest. Then 1 more bear came by. How many bears were there altogether?

 There were 4 bears that were looking for honey. Two more bears joined them. How many bears were looking for honey?

 Five bears were playing in the grass. Then 2 bears climbed a tree. How many bears were left in the grass?

- Continue with other word problems until the cup is empty.

Looking at Letters and Words

Language Arts Standard: *Begins to identify onsets and rimes*

- Duplicate the bear (p. 43) on brown construction paper and cut it out. Reduce the bear to a smaller size, if desired. Provide one bear for each child.
- Write each child's name on one side of a bear and stick a small piece of magnetic or double-sided tape on the back. Put all of the bears in a bowl or basket.
- Pull out one bear at a time from the basket. Say the name on the bear, separating the onset and rime. For example, say *This name begins with /k/ and ends with /atie/.*
- Invite children to blend the sounds together and say the name.
- Have children put their bear on the board or magnetic board when their name is said.
- If desired, use the bears with other activities that involve name recognition.

Real Bears vs. Storybook Bears

Language Arts Standard: *Communicates information with others*

- Show children a book about a storybook bear and a book about a real bear.

- Lead a discussion with them about the difference between what real bears do and what storybook bears do.

- Create a T-chart on the board that contrasts real bears and bear characters found in stories.

- Invite children to tell what they know about bears and write their responses on the chart.

Real Bears	Storybook Bears
live in the woods	live in houses
can be dangerous	are friendly
growl	talk
have furry coats	wear clothing

In Tune with Language

Language Arts Standard: *Listens with understanding and responds to directions*

- Invite children to hold a teddy bear and participate in the following chant.

Teddy bear, teddy bear, jump up and down.
Teddy bear, teddy bear, turn all around.
Teddy bear, teddy bear, touch the ground.
Teddy bear, teddy bear, turn out the light.
Teddy bear, teddy bear, say "Goodnight."

- Challenge children to think of other movements their teddy bear can do.

Sensational Seasons: Fall, SV 9781419033957

Let's Write: Dear Teddy Bear

Language Arts Standard: *Understands that different texts such as letters, notes, or lists are used for different purposes*

- Have children help create a letter that invites their teddy bear to visit their school. Ask children to bring a teddy bear from home if they have one. Have a few extra teddy bears for children who do not have one at home or forget to bring theirs.

- Write the invitation on chart paper for children to see. Explain that a letter begins with a greeting such as *Dear Teddy Bear.*

- Have them look on the class calendar to determine the date for the visit.

- Have children follow along as you read the letter. Then reproduce it to send home.

- Invite children to sign their letter with their name and decorate it with crayons and stickers.

> Dear Teddy Bear,
>
> Please come visit me at school on Friday, September 6.
>
> Love,
> Joseph

Bears on Parade

Language Arts Standard: *Listens with understanding and responds to directions*

- Provide each child with one-half of a graham cracker, a tablespoon of chocolate cake icing, and four tiny bear cookies.

- Invite children to completely cover the graham cracker with the chocolate icing using a plastic knife.

- Have children stand the bears in the icing in a row.

- Challenge children to point to the first bear, the second bear, and so on.

- Have them tell which bear they are going to eat first, such as *I am going to eat the fourth bear first.*

- Invite children to eat their bears in the order they described.

Caution: Be aware of children who may have food allergies.

Bears: Writing Activity and Snack Idea
Sensational Seasons: Fall, SV 9781419033957

Math Center

Math Standard:
Counts objects using one-to-one correspondence

Honey Pots

- Duplicate ten honey pots (p. 44). Color and cut them out. Write a number from 1 to 10 on the honey section of each pot. Laminate them for durability.
- Provide children with a large supply of plastic counting bears.
- Invite children to count out the designated number of bears on each honey pot.
- For younger children, draw dots on the honey pot to correspond with the number on the honey section. Have them match one bear to each dot.

Language Center

Language Arts Standard:
Recognizes and names letters of the alphabet

Bear Tracks

- Duplicate and cut out paw prints (p. 44) on brown construction paper. The number of paw prints will be determined by the space available in the classroom.
- Write a letter of the alphabet on each paw print. You may wish to include all twenty-six letters or just several target letters. Laminate them for durability.
- Tape the paw prints on the floor, starting at the entrance to the classroom. Place them in a winding path that ends at the language center.
- Place a bowl or basket of honeycomb-shaped cereal at the end of the path.
- Lead a discussion with children about how bears love honey, which is made by bees and stored in beehives.
- Invite children to pretend they are bears looking for honey.
- Have them follow the bear tracks and name each letter as they step on the paw prints.
- Invite children to eat a spoonful of honeycomb-shaped cereal at the end of the path.

Caution: Be aware of children who may have food allergies.

Sensational Seasons: Fall, SV 9781419033957

Art Center

Art Standard:
Explores a variety of
techniques to create
original work

A Chocolate Teddy Bear

- Duplicate the bear (p. 43) for use as a template. Enlarge the bear, if desired. Cut it out and trace a bear shape on finger-paint paper for each child.

- Prepare chocolate pudding according to directions. Mix in a few tablespoons of coffee grounds to give the pudding a rough texture.

- Invite children to use their fingers to paint their bear with the pudding and coffee grounds mixture.

- Have them glue on two wiggly eyes, a black pom-pom nose, and a piece of red rickrack for a mouth.

- Then have children glue two or three buttons on the tummy to complete the teddy bear.

Caution: Be aware of children who may have food allergies.

Sensory Center

Language Arts
Standard:
Stays with or repeats
a task

Floating Bears

- Put 20 or 30 plastic bear counters that float and a large spoon in the water tub.

- Invite children to scoop up the bear counters with the spoon.

- Have them count how many bears were in the spoon. Set those bears aside.

- Have children continue scooping up and counting the bears until the tub has no more bears.

- As a variation, have children name the colors of the bears in each scoop.

Sensational Seasons: Fall, SV 9781419033957

Bear Pattern

Use with "Our Cuddly Cubs" on page 37, "Looking at Letters and Words"
on page 38, and "A Chocolate Teddy Bear" on page 42.

bear

Sensational Seasons: Fall, SV 9781419033957

Honey Pot Pattern

Use with "Honey Pots" on page 41.

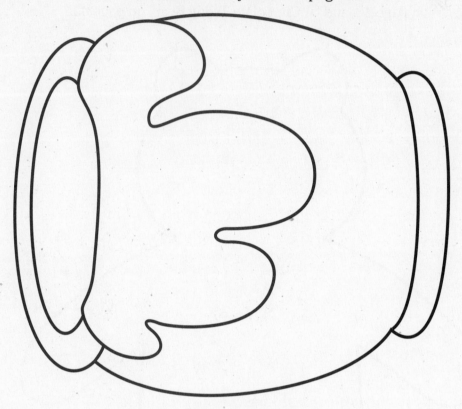

honey pot

Bear Paw Pattern

Use with "Bear Tracks" on page 41.

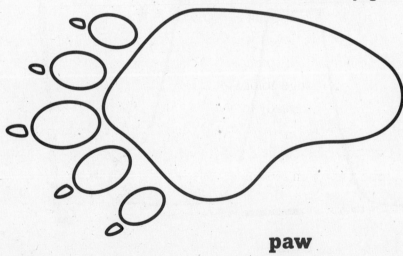

paw

Picking Pumpkins

Books to Read

Big Pumpkin by Erica Silverman (Aladdin)

I Like Pumpkins by Jerry Smath (Cartwheel Books)

It's Pumpkin Time! by Zoe Hall (Scholastic)

Patty's Pumpkin Patch by Teri Sloat (Putnam Juvenile)

Pumpkin Day, Pumpkin Night by Anne Rockwell (Walker & Company)

Pumpkin, Pumpkin by Jeanne Titherington (HarperTrophy)

The Pumpkin Book by Gail Gibbons (Holiday House)

The Ugly Pumpkin by Dave Horowitz (Putnam Juvenile)

Too Many Pumpkins by Linda White (Holiday House)

Pumpkin Facts

Pumpkins are believed to have originated in Central America as far back as 6000 B.C. The word *pumpkin* comes from the Greek word *pepon*, which means "large melon." A pumpkin is a fruit that is 90 percent water and is a good source of potassium and vitamin A. A leafy vine grows from a pumpkin seed, and yellowish orange flowers bloom on the vine. If pollination occurs, the ovaries at the base of the flower will swell and become tiny green pumpkins. The pumpkins continue to grow large and begin to change color. About four months after planting, they are ready to harvest. Pumpkins can vary in color from white to yellow to orange. The orange Connecticut field variety is the traditional pumpkin eaten in the United States.

Pumpkins: Book List and Teacher Information
Sensational Seasons: Fall, SV 9781419033957

Pumpkin Pickin' Time

Materials

- brown and green craft paper
- border
- yellow tissue paper
- paper plates
- green construction paper
- green pipe cleaners
- orange tempera paint
- paintbrushes
- markers
- scissors
- tape
- stapler
- pencils

Directions

Teacher Preparation: Cover the bulletin board with brown craft paper. Cut the green craft paper into sections that are one foot wide and several feet long. Twist these pieces to resemble pumpkin vines and staple them in a random order on the bulletin board. Cut green leaves and staple them to the vines. Cut three-inch squares of yellow tissue paper and twist them to resemble a blossom. Staple them to the vines. Add a border and the caption.

1. Paint the bottom side of the paper plate orange. Allow it to dry.

2. Draw and cut out a stem from a small piece of green construction paper.

3. Tape the stem on the unpainted side of the plate.

4. Wrap a green pipe cleaner around a pencil to make a spiral.

5. Tape the spiral next to the stem.

6. Draw a few vertical lines on the plate with a dark marker to make the pumpkin ribs.

7. Staple the pumpkins on the vines in a pleasing arrangement.

Guess What?

Language Arts Standard: *Predicts what will happen next using pictures and content for guides*

- Before class starts and out of sight of the children, put an orange basketball inside a grocery bag. Set a medium-sized pumpkin somewhere in the classroom.

- Place the bag in an area where children can sit around it. Invite children to sit around the grocery bag.

- Tell them that you are going to give them clues about what is inside the bag. Say the following riddle.

  I am orange. I am round.
  I have lines that go up and down.
  If you touch me, I feel rough.
  That's all of my clues. That's enough.

- Have children tell what they think is in the bag. Most children will guess a pumpkin.

- Remove the basketball from the bag and compare it to the pumpkin.

- Challenge children to think of other clues that help distinguish the pumpkin from the ball such as *I have a stem, I can bounce,* or *I can be eaten.*

Pick a Pumpkin

Language Arts Standard: *Recognizes and names rhyming words*

- Use the completed pumpkins from "Paper Bag Pumpkins" on page 51 to make a pumpkin patch. Tape a picture of a rhyming word on the bottom of each bag. Then set the bags in random order on a rug.

- Invite children to sit around the pumpkin patch.

- Have them "pick" a pumpkin and look at the picture on the bottom.

- Challenge them to name a word that rhymes with their picture.

- Make a list on the board of the words the children named. Have them follow along as you read the rhyming words.

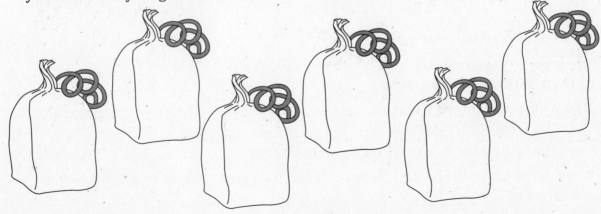

Sensational Seasons: Fall, SV 9781419033957

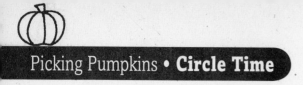

Pass the Pumpkin

Math Standard: *Names common shapes*

- Cut out a few circles, squares, triangles, and rectangles from construction paper. Laminate them for durability. Provide each child with a shape. Put the shapes in a plastic pumpkin or a lunch sack with a pumpkin drawn on it.

- Have children sit in a circle and sing the following song to the tune of "Frère Jacques" as they pass the pumpkin around the circle.

  Pass the pumpkin. Pass the pumpkin.
  Round and round. Round and round.
  When it stops. When it stops,
  Name the shape you found. Name the shape you found.

- Invite the child who is holding the pumpkin when the word *stops* is sung to pick a shape from the pumpkin.

- Have the child name the shape.

- Continue passing the pumpkin until all children have had a turn picking a shape from the pumpkin and naming the shape.

In Tune with Language

Language Arts Standard: *Recognizes and names rhyming words*

- Invite children to learn the following song to the tune of "Twinkle, Twinkle, Little Star."

  Little pumpkin on the vine
  How I wish that you were mine.

  You grow bigger every day
  Turning orange along the way.

  Now a big pumpkin can be found.
  There it is right on the ground.

- Have children name the rhyming words in each verse.

- Write the words on the board. Challenge children to think of other words that rhyme with those in the song.

Let's Write: Sand Letters

Language Arts Standard: *Writes to produce letters of the alphabet*

- Write the word *pumpkin* on a sentence strip. Use uppercase letters for younger children.

- Write the individual letters of the word *pumpkin* on index cards. Arrange them in the correct sequence to spell the word *pumpkin*.

- Put a thin layer of sand on a tray.

- Invite children to use their finger to write the letters in the word one at a time in the correct order in the sand.

- Encourage children to use the letter cards as a model.

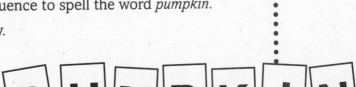

Mini-Pumpkin Pies

Language Arts Standard: *Understands that letters make sounds*

- Provide a can of pumpkin pie mix, two-thirds cup of evaporated milk, one-half cup of sugar, two beaten eggs, and a package of pre-made pie crust dough.

- Spray a mini-muffin tin with non-stick spray.

- Provide children with a two-inch ball of pie crust dough. Invite them to press it into the mini-muffin tin and make a "bowl" shape.

- Invite children to mix the pumpkin mix, evaporated milk, sugar, and eggs in a bowl.

- Have children spoon a small amount of the pumpkin pie filling into their crust.

- Bake according to crust package directions until crust is brown.

- If desired, have children add a dab of whipped topping on the "pie."

- Challenge children to think of alliterative sentences such as *Please pass the pumpkin pie.*

Caution: Be aware of children who may have food allergies.

Sensational Seasons: Fall, SV 9781419033957

Math Center

Math Standard:
Uses concepts that include number recognition and counting

Pumpkin Clips

- Duplicate ten pumpkins and stems (p. 53) on orange and green construction paper. Cut them out.

- Write a number from 1 to 10 on the stems. Laminate the stems for durability. Glue each stem on a spring clothespin.

- Draw dots on the pumpkins from 1 to 10. Laminate the pumpkins for durability.

- Invite children to attach the clothespins to the pumpkins with the corresponding number of dots.

Language Center

Language Arts Standard:
Retells a story in sequence using illustrations

From Seed to Pumpkin

- Duplicate the cards (p. 52) for each child. Provide each child with a half sheet of construction paper for use as a book cover.

- Read a book from the list on page 45 that includes the life cycle of the pumpkin plant. Discuss with children how a pumpkin plant grows. Use the cards to demonstrate the sequence.

- Invite children to retell how the pumpkin plant grows by putting the cards in the correct sequence.

- Help children staple the cards in sequence to make a book. Then have the children fold the construction paper around the cards to make a front and back cover.

- Have children color the pictures and decorate the front cover.

Art Center

Art Standard:
Explores a variety of tools to create original work

Paper Bag Pumpkins

- Set up a paint center with orange and green tempera paint.
- Duplicate a spiral vine (p. 53) on green construction paper for each child.
- Provide children with a lunch sack, a rubber band, and some sheets of newspaper.
- Have children stuff the lunch sack two-thirds full with crumpled newspaper. Help them twist the top of the sack to make a stem and secure it with a rubber band.
- Invite children to paint the stuffed part of the sack orange and the "stem" green. Set aside to dry.
- Have children cut out the spiral vine. Younger children may need help with cutting.
- Glue the vine to the stem to complete the pumpkin.

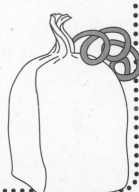

What's Inside?

Sensory Center

Science Standard:
Uses senses to observe and explore materials

- Provide children with a large pumpkin, safety goggles, a toy hammer, and a generous supply of golf tees.
- Have children decide on a face to draw on the pumpkin. Draw the face using a permanent marker.
- Invite children to hammer the golf tees into the pumpkin using the face lines drawn on it as a guide.
- When the face is completed, have an adult cut the top off the pumpkin.
- Have children remove the seeds and pulp. Discuss how the inside of the pumpkin looks, feels, and smells. If desired, have children taste the raw pumpkin.
- Encourage children to remove the golf tees.
- Place a small flashlight inside the pumpkin, replace the top, and turn off the lights to see the pumpkin face.

Caution: Be aware of children who may have food allergies.

Sensational Seasons: Fall, SV 9781419033957

Life Cycle Cards

Use with "From Seed to Pumpkin" on page 50.

Pumpkins: Life Cycle Cards
Sensational Seasons: Fall, SV 9781419033957

Pumpkin and Stem Patterns
Use with "Pumpkin Clips" on page 50.

pumpkin

stem

Vine Pattern
Use with "Paper Bag Pumpkins" on page 51.

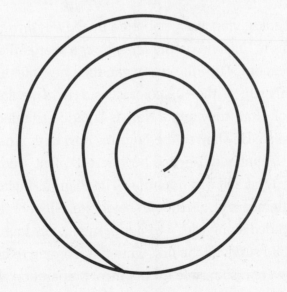

vine

Pumpkins: Patterns
Sensational Seasons: Fall, SV 9781419033957

Thanksgiving: Then and Now

Books to Read

Arthur's Thanksgiving by Marc Brown (Little, Brown & Company)

How Many Days to America?: A Thanksgiving Story by Eve Bunting (Clarion Books)

Thanksgiving at Our House by Wendy Watson (Clarion Books)

Thanksgiving Is for Giving Thanks by Margaret Sutherland (Grosset & Dunlap)

Thanksgiving Mice by Bethany Roberts (Clarion Books)

Thank You, Thanksgiving by David Milgrim (Clarion Books)

The Night Before Thanksgiving by Natasha Wing (Grosset & Dunlap)

The Pilgrims' First Thanksgiving by Ann McGovern (Scholastic)

Turkey Surprise by Peggy Archer (Dial Books)

'Twas the Night Before Thanksgiving by Dav Pilkey (Scholastic)

Thanksgiving Facts

The first Thanksgiving was celebrated by the Pilgrims in 1621. They had sailed from England on the *Mayflower* a year earlier in search of religious freedom. The Pilgrims began their new life in the Plymouth Colony. Only half of the 102 colonists survived the first harsh winter. In March of 1621, they met a Native American named Squanto who spoke English. He showed the Pilgrims how to tap maple trees for sap, how to hunt and fish, and how best to plant seeds. As a result, the harvest that fall was bountiful. The Pilgrims invited Squanto and the members of his tribe to celebrate. Ninety men from the tribe attended along with 41 Pilgrim men. Only four Pilgrim women had survived the first winter. According to custom, the women were responsible for the meal preparation and were not invited. The celebration lasted for three days.

Sensational Seasons: Fall, SV 9781419033957

We Give Thanks

Materials

- blue and brown craft paper
- border
- manila paper
- black, white, yellow, light brown, pink, red, green, and orange tempera paint
- paintbrushes
- small paper plates
- markers
- scissors
- stapler

Directions

Teacher Preparation: Cover the bulletin board with blue craft paper. Cut out a large brown rectangle for a table. Staple the table across the bottom of the bulletin board. Add the caption and a border. Set up a paint center.

1. Discuss with children how the Pilgrims and Native Americans celebrated the first Thanksgiving together.

2. Invite children to paint a large Pilgrim or Native American head on manila paper. Have children include the hat and collar for the Pilgrim and a headband with feathers for the Native American. Allow paintings to dry.

3. Have children cut out their Pilgrim or Native American and add facial features with markers.

4. Have children use markers to draw pictures of food on a small paper plate.

5. Staple the faces around the table on the bulletin board. Staple the plates on the table in front of the children's faces.

The Pilgrims on the Mayflower

Language Arts Standard: *Begins to distinguish letters in written text*

- Read a book or tell children the story about how the Pilgrims came to America on the *Mayflower* in search of religious freedom. See the Thanksgiving Facts on page 54.
- Write the words *Pilgrims* and *Mayflower* in large print on copy paper. Make two copies for each child.
- Provide each child with a copy of the paper with the two words written on it.
- Cut apart the letters in the words on the second copy to make a set of individual letters. Give each child a set of letters in a plastic zipper bag.
- Challenge children to match the letters in the bag to the ones on their paper to spell the words *Pilgrims* and *Mayflower*.
- Invite them to glue the letters on their paper.

Across the Ocean

Language Arts Standard: *Recognizes and names rhyming words*

- Duplicate a ticket (p. 61) for each child. Duplicate a rhyming picture card (pages 6–8) for each ticket. Cut out the pictures and glue one on each ticket.
- In a large open area, make an imaginary ship by setting chairs in rows of four with an aisle down the middle.
- Explain that the Pilgrims had to have a ticket to sail on the *Mayflower*. Give each child a ticket.
- Invite children to form a line to prepare to board the ship. Have them name a word that rhymes with the picture on their "ticket" as they hand it to you.
- Have children sit in a chair on the "ship."
- When all children are on board, stand in front of them and read a book about the Pilgrims that describes their journey on the *Mayflower*.

Favorite Thanksgiving Foods

Math Standard: *Represents data using concrete objects, pictures, and graphs*

- Read a book that tells about the foods that were eaten at the first Thanksgiving.
- Have children name four or five foods that are commonly eaten at Thanksgiving now. Guide younger children since they may not have a frame of reference for Thanksgiving yet.
- Make a large graph with four or five columns. Draw pictures of the foods named at the top of the columns.
- Duplicate the children's class photos and glue them on index cards.
- Invite children to tape their photo on the graph below their favorite Thanksgiving food.

Sensational Seasons: Fall, SV 9781419033957

Looking at Letters and Words

Language Arts Standard: *Demonstrates some ability to hear separate syllables in words*

- Write the word *thankful* on the board. Have children tell what words they hear in the word *thankful* (*thank* and *ful*).
- Invite children to say the word slowly and segment the syllables (*thank-ful*).
- Have them clap the syllables as they say them and then blend the word *thankful* back together.
- Encourage children to clap and count the syllables for other words such as *Thanksgiving, corn, celebration, family, Pilgrim,* and *turkey*.

In Tune with Language

Language Arts Standard: *Understands that different texts such as letters, notes, or lists are used for different purposes*

- Invite children to learn the following song to the tune of "Do You Know the Muffin Man?"

  I am thankful for my friends, for my friends, for my friends.

  I am thankful for my friends, on Thanksgiving Day.

- Have children repeat the verse, substituting other things they are thankful for such as their family, the trees, or good food.
- Write a list on the board of the things children are thankful for.
- Encourage children to follow along as you read the list.

Sensational Seasons: Fall, SV 9781419033957

Let's Write: We Are Thankful

Language Arts Standard: *Makes illustrations to match sentences*

- Have children write or dictate a sentence telling something that they are thankful for such as _____ *is thankful for* _____.

- Have them write their name on the first blank space and what they are thankful for on the second blank.

- You may wish to use the list of responses from children that tells what they are thankful for in the *In Tune with Language* activity on page 57.

- Invite children to draw a picture that illustrates their sentence.

Cornbread Muffins

Math Standard: *Uses measuring implements*

- Lead a discussion with children about how corn was planted and harvested by the Pilgrims. If possible, show them a real ear of corn and some cornmeal.

- Prepare a cooking station with a mixing bowl, a spoon, a muffin pan, and some paper muffin liners.

- Gather together a package of cornbread mix, one beaten egg, and two-thirds cup of milk. You may need to double the recipe depending on the number of children in your class.

- Invite children to measure the ingredients and mix them in a bowl until well blended.

- Have children line the muffin pan with paper liners.

- Have children spoon the mixture into the muffin pan.

- Bake according to package directions.

- Eat the muffins as part of a class Thanksgiving feast.

Caution: Be aware of children who may have food allergies.

Math Center

Math Standard:
Uses concepts that include number recognition and counting

Land, Ho!

- Duplicate the game board (p. 62) and write a number from 1 to 6 in each section. Repeat numbers in random order. Color the *START* and *FINISH* sections brown and color the rest of the board blue. Glue the game board to construction paper or a file folder and laminate.

- Construct a game piece by making a thumb indention in a one-and-a-half-inch ball of clay. Glue a one-inch square of white paper to a toothpick for a sail. Insert the toothpick in the clay and allow the clay to harden.

- Put the game board, game piece, and a number cube on the table.

- Explain to children that the Pilgrims left England and sailed to America on a ship called the *Mayflower*.

- Have children roll the number cube and move the ship to the corresponding number.

- Have children continue rolling the cube until they land in America.

Language Center

Language Arts Standard:
Begins to recognize high-frequency words

Ship Shape Words

- Lead a discussion with children about how the Pilgrims came to America on a ship called the *Mayflower*.

- Duplicate several ships (p. 61) on white construction paper. Color each ship brown and leave the sail white. Cut them out.

- Write a different high-frequency word such as *I, the,* and *is* on the sail of each of the ships. Laminate the ships for durability and stick a piece of magnetic tape on the back of each one.

- Put the ships on a table with a set of magnetic letters and a cookie sheet.

- Invite children to put one ship on the cookie sheet and use the magnetic letters to spell the word written on the ship.

Sensational Seasons: Fall, SV 9781419033957

Art Center

Art Standard:
Explores a variety of techniques to create original work

Pilgrim Centerpieces

- Duplicate a hat (p. 63) on white construction paper for each girl. Duplicate a hat (p. 63) on black construction paper for each boy. Duplicate a collar (p. 63) on white construction paper for each child.

- Have children stuff a lunch bag with newspaper. Help them staple the top closed.

- Have children trace a coffee can lid on pink or tan construction paper and cut it out.

- Invite children to draw a face and hair on the circle with markers or crayons and glue it on the bag.

- Have children cut out the hat and collar and glue them on the bag to complete the Pilgrim's face.

- Have the boys glue a small square of yellow paper on their hat for a buckle.

- Invite children to use their Pilgrims as a centerpiece at Thanksgiving dinner.

Sensory Center

Math Standard:
Demonstrates a beginning understanding of measurement

Corn and More Corn

- Lead a discussion with children about Squanto, who was one of the first Native American friends to the Pilgrims. Squanto taught the Pilgrims how to plant corn, beans, and other vegetables.

- If possible, show children an ear of Indian corn.

- Fill the sensory tub with deer corn and dried beans. Also put measuring cups and spoons in the tub.

- Invite children to pour and measure the corn and beans.

- Challenge children to discover how many little cups it takes to fill a big cup, and so on.

Ticket Pattern

Use with "Across the Ocean" on page 56.

ticket

Ship Pattern

Use with "Ship Shape Words" on page 59.

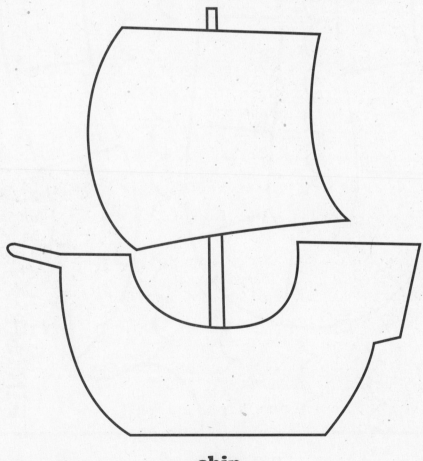

ship

Sensational Seasons: Fall, SV 9781419033957

Game Board
Use with "Land, Ho!" on page 59.

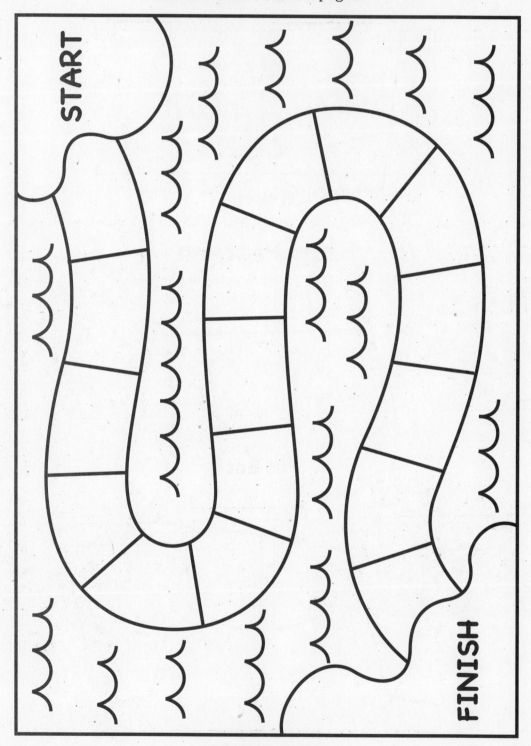

game board

Pilgrim Patterns
Use with "Pilgrim Centerpieces" on page 60.

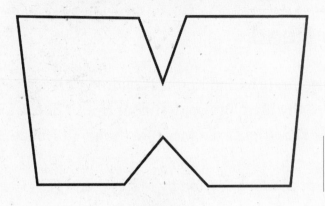

collar

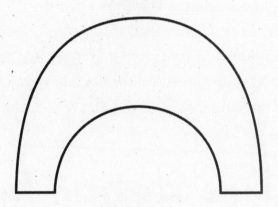

girl hat

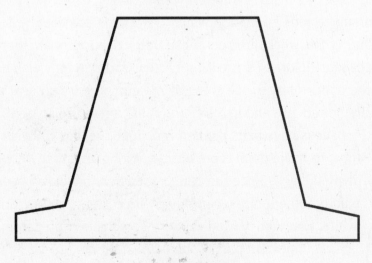

boy hat

Sensational Seasons: Fall, SV 9781419033957

Books to Read

A Day with Firefighters by Jan Kottke (Children's Press)

Arthur's Fire Drill by Marc Brown (Random House Books for Young Readers)

Big Frank's Fire Truck by Leslie McGuire (Random House Books for Young Readers)

Curious George at the Fire Station by Margret and H. A. Rey (Houghton Mifflin)

Fire! Fire! by Gail Gibbons (HarperTrophy)

Firefighters A to Z by Chris L. Demarest (Margaret K. McElderry)

I Want to Be a Firefighter by Dan Liebman (Firefly Books)

No Dragons for Tea by Jean Pendziwol (Kids Can Press, Ltd.)

Stop Drop and Roll by Margery Cuyler (Simon & Schuster Children's Publishing)

Fire Station Facts

Fire Prevention Day is October 9, the anniversary of the Great Chicago Fire in 1871. Fire Prevention Week is the Saturday through Sunday period in which October 9 falls each year. During this week, firetrucks visit many schools in an effort to educate children on fire safety rules. Children may also have the opportunity to see some of the equipment and gear that firefighters use and to learn about life at the fire station. Firetrucks have been painted red since the late 1920s in an effort to make them more visible among cars that were all painted black. Since the 1960s, firetrucks have also been painted other colors, particularly lime green, yellow, and white. Emergency Medical Service vehicles and paramedics are an important part of local fire stations.

FIRE STATION

Our Preschool Firefighters

Materials

- fire hat pattern (p. 71)
- blue craft paper
- border
- white construction paper
- crayons or markers
- plastic lid from a large coffee can
- glue
- stapler
- scissors

Directions

Teacher Preparation: Enlarge the fire hat to the size of the plastic lid. Duplicate a hat for each child. Cover the bulletin board with blue craft paper. Add a border and the caption.

1. Invite children to trace the plastic lid to make a circle in the center of the white paper. Younger children may need help.

2. Have children draw features on the circle to resemble their own eyes, nose, mouth, and hair.

3. Have children color and cut out the fire hat.

4. Invite children to glue the fire hat on the head picture that they drew.

5. Encourage children to write or dictate a sentence below their picture that tells something they learned about firefighters or fire safety.

6. Staple the pictures in a pleasing arrangement on the bulletin board.

Learning About the Fire Station

Language Arts Standard: *Relates prior knowledge to new information*

- Make a KWL chart showing three columns. Write KNOW, WANT, and LEARNED as headers for each column.
- Have children tell things they know about fire safety, firetrucks, firefighters, or a fire station. Write their responses in the KNOW column.
- Write things they want to know about the fire topics in the WANT column. Guide children to ask questions such as *Why do firefighters wear masks?*
- Read children an informational book from the book list on page 64 about fire-related topics. You may wish to plan a field trip to a fire station or invite local firefighters to visit the school.
- Invite children to complete the LEARNED column of the chart by telling things that they learned about the fire topics after reading the book or visiting the fire station.

Calling 911

Math Standard: *Recognizes and names numbers*

- Provide two toy phones or real phones that have been disconnected. Write each child's address on a sentence strip.
- Lead a discussion with children about the emergency number 911. Invite them to tell about situations that would make it necessary to call 911.
- Tell children that 911 operators need to know their address so that firefighters or paramedics will know where to go.
- Give each child his or her address card. Keep one phone and pretend you are the 911 operator. Have children take turns using the second phone to dial 911.
- Ask them to tell you their address when you "answer" the phone.
- Encourage children to read the numbers on their address. Help them with the street or road name as needed.

Looking at Letters and Words

Language Arts Standard: *Understands that reading progresses from left to right*

- Write the word *fire* on the board, naming each letter as it is written. Have children identify the beginning sound /f/.
- Write the following words on sentence strips: *fire house, fire station, fire dog, fire safety, firefighter, firetruck*.
- Put the word cards in a pocket chart.
- Have children help read the words beginning with the word *fire*. Point to each word as it is read, emphasizing left to right progression.

Put Out the Fire

Language Arts Standard: *Begins to understand and name opposites*

- Duplicate a flame (p. 71) for each child. Color the flames using orange, red, and yellow crayons. Write a word on each flame that has an opposite, such as *hot, off,* or *big.* Cut out the flames and laminate them. Stick a piece of magnetic tape on the back of each flame.

- Draw a house or building with several windows on a magnetic board. The size of the windows should match the size of the flames, and the number of windows will depend on the size of the board.

- Place one flame in each window of the building. Save the extras.

- Cut a two-foot section off the end of an old water hose. Attach a water spray nozzle. Wrap a piece of magnetic tape around the end of the nozzle.

- Invite children to hold the hose and touch the nozzle to one of the flames to put out the fire. The magnetic tape on the hose will attract the flame.

- Have children name the word that is the opposite of the one written on the flame.

- Repeat the activity using the additional flames until each child has had a turn.

In Tune with Language

Language Arts Standard: *Begins to distinguish words in sentences*

- Lead a discussion with children about what it means to have a fire drill. Younger children may need reassurance that a fire drill does not mean there is a real fire.

- Write the words *fire drill* on a sentence strip. Then write the words to the following song on a chart.

We practice what to do,	**Then we go outside,**
We practice what to do.	**Then we go outside.**
When we have a fire drill,	**When we have a fire drill,**
We practice what to do.	**Then we go outside.**
First we line up,	**We find our meeting place,**
First we line up.	**We find our meeting place.**
When we have a fire drill,	**When we have a fire drill,**
First we line up.	**We find our meeting place.**

- Invite children to sing the song to the tune of "Hi-Ho the Derry-O."

- Challenge children to look at the words *fire drill* on the sentence strip and find them in each verse of the song.

Let's Write: Don't Touch Matches!

Language Arts Standard: *Makes illustrations to match sentences*

- Show children real matches. Have them tell what they know about matches and why it is important that they never play with or even touch matches.

- Have them write or dictate a response to complete the sentence frame *If I found matches, I would* _____.

- Invite them to use crayons or markers to illustrate their sentence.

Firefighter Ladder and Hose

Language Arts Standard: *Shows awareness that different words begin with the same sound*

- Gather together six-inch pretzel sticks, small pretzel sticks, spreadable cream cheese, red licorice strings, and paper plates.

- Invite children to make a ladder by laying two six-inch pretzel sticks on a plate so they are about two inches apart.

- Have children dip each end of five small pretzel sticks in the cream cheese. Then have children lay the pretzels perpendicular to the long pretzels to make the rungs of the ladder.

- Have children wrap one string of licorice around two fingers to make a coiled hose. Lay the hose beside the ladder.

- Challenge children to name the beginning sound for the words *ladder* and *hose* and name other words that begin with those sounds.

Caution: Be aware of children who may have food allergies.

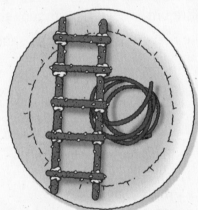

Math Center

Math Standard:
Uses concepts that include number recognition and counting

Dot the Fire House Dog

- Duplicate ten dogs (p. 71) on white construction paper. Draw large black dots on the ears, with each dog having from 1 to 10 dots. Divide the number of dots as evenly as possible between the two ears, such as 3 dots on one ear and 2 dots on the other for the number 5. Cut out and laminate the dogs.

- Duplicate ten fire hats (p. 71) on white construction paper. Color the badge area yellow and the hat red. Write numbers from 1 to 10 on the yellow badges. Cut out and laminate them.

- Invite children to count the dots on the ears and put the hat with the corresponding number on the dog's head.

Language Center

Language Arts Standard:
Matches partner letters

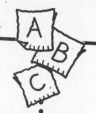

Fire Hydrant Hook-Ups

- Gather 8 to 10 empty thread spools. Paint them white, yellow, or red to match the color of fire hydrants. Write a target uppercase letter on each "fire hydrant" spool.

- Duplicate one hose nozzle (p. 71) on gray construction paper for each spool. Write partner letters on the nozzles. Cut them out and laminate them.

- Cut thick, black pipe cleaners in half and loosely wrap them around two fingers to form a fire hose. Tape a nozzle on the end of each "hose."

- Challenge children to match the uppercase letters on the "fire hydrants" with the correct partner letters on the nozzles of the "fire hoses." Invite children to "hook-up" each "hose" to the correct "hydrant" by putting the end of the pipe cleaner into the hole in the spool.

Art Center

Art Standard:
Explores a variety of
techniques to create
original work

Squeeze Bottle Art

- Duplicate a firetruck (p. 72) on red construction paper for each child.

- Fill three squeeze bottles with red, yellow, and white tempera paint.

- Provide each child with a sheet of black construction paper and a sheet of waxed paper that are the same size.

- Invite children to squeeze all three colors of paint on the black paper. Caution children that applying too much paint will saturate the paper.

- Have children place the waxed paper on top of the painted black paper. Have them rub across the waxed paper with the edge of a jumbo craft stick to spread the paint.

- Have children gently pull off the waxed paper and discard it. Allow the paint to dry.

- Invite children to cut out the firetruck and glue it on the "fire" painting.

Sensory Center

Science Standard:
Uses senses to observe
and explore materials

Put Out the Fire!

- Lead a discussion with children about how fireboats are used to put out fires on watercraft or structures on or near the water.

- Put several toy boats in a water tub.

- Fill two or three spray bottles with water.

- Invite children to use the spray bottles to put out "fires" on the boats. Tell children that they should spray only the boats.

Sensational Seasons: Fall, SV 9781419033957

Flame Pattern
Use with "Put Out the Fire" on page 67.

Nozzle Pattern
Use with "Fire Hydrant Hook-Ups" on page 69.

flame

nozzle

Hat and Dog Patterns
Use with "Our Preschool Firefighters" on page 65 and "Dot the Fire House Dog" on page 69.

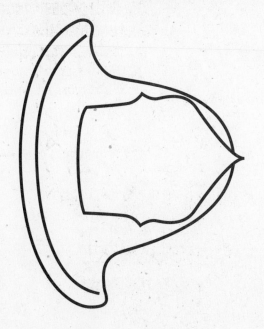

fire hat

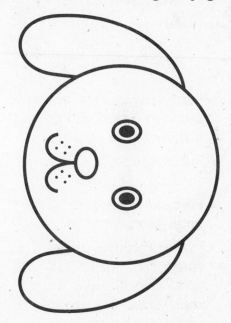

dog

Sensational Seasons: Fall, SV 9781419033957

Firetruck Pattern
Use with "Squeeze Bottle Art" on page 70.

firetruck

Sensational Seasons: Fall, SV 9781419033957

Looking at Leaves

Books to Read

A Simple Brown Leaf by L. J. Davis (Abovo Publishing)

Autumn Leaves by Ken Robbins (Scholastic Trade)

Fall Leaves by Mary Packard (Cartwheel)

Fall Leaves Fall! by Zoe Hall (Scholastic Press)

I Am a Leaf by Jean Marzollo (Cartwheel)

I Found a Leaf by Sharon Lerner (Lerner Publishing Group)

Leaf Man by Lois Ehlert (Harcourt Children's Books)

Leaves! Leaves! Leaves! by Nancy Elizabeth Wallace (Marshall Cavendish Corp.)

Red Leaf, Yellow Leaf by Lois Ehlert (Harcourt Children's Books)

Why Do Leaves Change Color? by Betsy Maestro (HarperTrophy)

Leaf Facts

Leaves produce food for trees and plants by combining water, carbon dioxide from the air, sunlight, and something inside the leaves called chlorophyll. All of these things combined make a special sugar that is food for the plants and trees. Chlorophyll is green, but the leaves also have orange and yellow inside them. During the summer, chlorophyll is busy making food and covers up the other colors. In preparation for winter, the plants and trees grow a thin layer of cells that cut off the water supply into the leaves. The chlorophyll stops making food, and the green disappears from the leaves, allowing the other colors to be seen. Sometimes the sugar gets trapped in the leaves, causing the leaves to turn red or purple. When the leaves die, they turn brown.

Leaves: Book List and Teacher Information
Sensational Seasons: Fall, SV 9781419033957

Fall Leaves Fall

Materials

- leaf pattern (p. 80)
- any color of craft paper
- border
- white construction paper
- damp sponges
- tempera paint in fall colors
- paintbrushes
- scissors
- stapler

Directions

Teacher Preparation: Duplicate the leaf on construction paper. Provide a copy for each child. Cover the bulletin board with craft paper. Draw or paint a large tree in the center of the bulletin board. Add a border and the caption. Set up a paint center.

1. Cut out the leaf pattern.

2. Use a sponge to paint the leaf using the fall colors.

3. Arrange and staple the leaves in a pleasing arrangement on the bulletin board.

The Green of Chlorophyll

Language Arts Standard: *Understands that reading progresses from left to right*

- Duplicate a large leaf (p. 80) on white construction paper.

- Use a sponge to paint the leaf with red, yellow, and orange paint. Allow the painted leaf to dry.

- Write the following facts about leaves on sentence strips and put them in a pocket chart.

  Leaves are green.
  Leaves are red.
  Leaves are yellow.
  Leaves are orange.

- Have children follow along as the words are read from left to right.

- Lead a discussion with children about how leaves have red, yellow, and orange colors in them. Explain that the colors cannot be seen during the summer when the leaves are making food for the plant or tree. Food is made for the leaves by chlorophyll, which is green in color. The green chlorophyll covers all of the other colors in the leaves. When cool weather arrives, the green color disappears to reveal the hidden colors.

- Show children the painted leaf. Point out the red, yellow, and orange colors.

- Demonstrate how the green chlorophyll covers up those colors by painting over the leaf with green paint.

Leaf Sounds

Language Arts Standard: *Demonstrates an understanding of letters and words*

- Enlarge the leaf pattern (p. 81) to twice the size. Duplicate 26 leaves on red, yellow, orange, and brown construction paper.

- Write an uppercase letter of the alphabet on each leaf. Cut out the leaves and laminate them.

- Spell a three-phoneme word such as *cat* by placing the leaf letters in a pocket chart.

- Point to each letter and have children say the sound it makes.

- Invite children to blend sounds together to say the word.

- Repeat the activity by changing a beginning, middle, or ending sound to make a new word.

Graphing Leaves

Math Standard: *Represents data using concrete objects, pictures, and graphs*

- Duplicate forty leaves (p. 81) and color ten brown, ten red, ten yellow, and ten orange. Cut out and laminate the leaves.

- Make a graph with four columns on a large sheet of paper. Glue one of each leaf color as headers for the columns.

- Put all of the remaining leaves in a bag or basket. Shake it to mix up the leaves.

- Invite children to pick one leaf from the container and name the color.

- Have children place their leaf in the correct column of the graph using double-sided tape.

- Encourage children to count how many leaves are in each column.

In Tune with Language

Language Arts Standard: *Participates in songs that emphasize sounds and rhymes*

- Invite children to sing the following song to the tune of "Do You Know the Muffin Man?"

See the leaves all falling down,
Falling down, falling down.
See the leaves all falling down,
Red, yellow, orange, and brown.

Look at all the leaves I found,
Leaves I found, leaves I found.
Look at all the leaves I found,
Lying on the ground.

- Challenge children to name words in the song that rhyme.

Let's Write: The Colors of Fall Leaves

Language Arts Standard: *Uses drawing and writing skills to convey meaning and information*

- Have children name all of the colors that are on fall leaves, including green, red, yellow, orange, brown, and purple. Write the color words on a chart.

- Duplicate a leaf (p. 80) on white construction paper for each child.

- Invite children to paint their leaf a fall color from the list on the chart.

- Have children complete the sentence frame *(Name)'s* _____ *leaf is* _____ on the construction paper.

- Challenge children to write their name and the color word in their sentence.

- Staple the pages together and add a cover to make a class book.

Leaf Cookies

Math Standard: *Represents data using concrete objects, pictures, and graphs*

- Provide children with a two-inch ball of sugar cookie dough.

- Have children roll out the dough and use a leaf-shaped cookie cutter to cut out one cookie each.

- Mix a few drops of red, yellow, and orange food coloring in separate bowls of milk.

- Invite children to use a clean paintbrush to paint their cookie with colored milk.

- Bake the cookies according to recipe directions.

- Make a graph with three columns, placing a red, yellow, and orange leaf at the top of each column. Cut out additional leaves from the same colors.

- Have children glue a leaf on the graph that matches the color of their cookie.

Caution: Be aware of children who may have food allergies.

Sensational Seasons: Fall, SV 9781419033957

Math Center

Math Standard:
Demonstrates a beginning understanding of measurement

Measuring Leaves

- Duplicate five leaves (p. 81) on red, yellow, or orange construction paper. Enlarge and reduce the leaves so that they are five distinct sizes. Cut them out and laminate them.

- Place a container of plastic interlocking cubes at the table with the leaves.

- Invite children to measure the leaves and count how many cubes long each leaf is.

- Encourage children to put the leaves in order from longest to shortest.

Language Center

Language Arts Standard:
Shows awareness that different words begin with the same sound

L Is for Leaf

- Draw or paint a brown tree on a large sheet of construction paper. Laminate it for durability.

- Duplicate eight leaves (p. 81) and color them fall colors on one side.

- Duplicate the picture cards (p. 81). Cut them out and glue one picture on the back of each leaf. Cut out the leaves and laminate them.

- Invite children to lay all of the leaves facedown on a table next to the tree.

- Have children name the beginning sound for the word *leaf*.

- Challenge them to turn over each leaf and identify the beginning sound in the name of each picture.

- Have children put the leaf on the tree if the name of the picture begins with the /l/ sound as in the word *leaf*.

- Have children put the leaf on the ground by the tree if the name of the picture begins with a different sound.

Art Center

Art Standard:
Explores a variety of materials to create original work

Sparkly Leaf Prints

- Invite children to go on a nature walk and collect leaves that are pliable and large.
- Have children select one leaf and paint the bottom side of the leaf a fall color.
- Have children cover the painted side of the leaf with white paper.
- Invite children to roll a rolling pin across the paper to make a leaf print on the paper.
- Have children gently lift the paper to reveal the leaf print.
- Have children sprinkle the leaf print with iridescent glitter while the paint is still wet.

Science Center

Science Standard:
Examines organisms by paying attention to detail

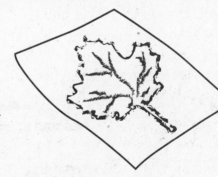

Take a Close Look

- Provide children with a variety of leaves that are different colors and shapes, a magnifying glass, newsprint, and crayons.
- Have children use the magnifying glass to look at the leaves.
- Invite children to make leaf rubbings using the newsprint and crayons.
- Point out that leaves have veins that feed plants just like people have veins that carry blood.

www.harcourtschoolsupply.com
© Harcourt Achieve Inc. All rights reserved.

Large Leaf Pattern

Use with "Fall Leaves Fall" on page 74, "The Green of Chlorophyll" on page 75,
and "The Colors of Fall Leaves" on page 77.

leaf

Sensational Seasons: Fall, SV 9781419033957

Small Leaf Pattern

Use with "Leaf Sounds" on page 75, "Graphing Leaves" on page 76,
"Measuring Leaves" on page 78, and "L Is for Leaf" on page 78.

leaf

Picture Cards

Use with "L Is for Leaf" on page 78.

Leaves: Pattern and Picture Cards
Sensational Seasons: Fall, SV 9781419033957

Books to Read

Brave Little Monster by Ken Baker (HarperCollins)

Five Ugly Monsters by Tedd Arnold (Cartwheel)

Glad Monster, Sad Monster by Anne Miranda (Little, Brown & Co.)

Go Away, Big Green Monster! by Ed Emberley (LB Kids)

Monster's Lunch Box by Marc Brown (Little, Brown & Co.)

The Boy Under the Bed by Preston McClear (Mailbu Books for Children)

There Are Monsters Everywhere by Mercer Mayer (Dial)

There's a Monster Under My Bed by James Howe (Aladdin)

Where the Wild Things Are by Maurice Sendak (HarperCollins)

Monster Facts

Monsters are imaginary creatures that are part human and part animal or made up of parts of two or more different animals. Tertology is the study of monsters. Things that are *monstrous* are huge. An enormous variety of monsters and beasts have appeared in mythologies and legends of ancient and modern cultures. Monsters have been part of children's literature throughout history. Cute monsters appear frequently in children's books so as not to be frightening but instead exciting and mildly scary. Children seem to enjoy the excitement as long as all is right at the end of the story.

Monster Museum

Materials

- any color craft paper
- border
- black construction paper
- variety of colors of construction paper
- scrap construction paper
- small paper cups
- chalk
- various craft supplies such as buttons, yarn, fabric, pom-poms, crinkled paper, and glitter
- markers
- glue
- scissors
- stapler
- tape

Directions

Teacher Preparation: Use a variety of colors to cut a supply of eight-inch circles and six-inch by eight-inch rectangles to be used as monster faces. Also cut out a generous supply of smaller circles, triangles, and squares. Cover the bulletin board with craft paper. Add a border and the caption.

1. Invite children to glue a large circle or a rectangle on black construction paper.

2. Have them use the various craft items to create a monster face.

3. Invite children to make their picture three-dimensional by gluing a paper cup on the face for a nose. Children may glue a pom-pom on the "nose" for a wart. You may also cut out half circles and help children make cone-shaped noses.

4. Have children sign their name on their artwork like an artist does using chalk on the black paper.

5. Staple the monsters in rows to resemble an art gallery.

Sensational Seasons: Fall, SV 9781419033957

Monster Stories

Language Arts Standard: *Retells information from a story*

- Select a monster story from the book list on page 82.
- Read the title aloud and tell children the name of the author and the illustrator.
- Point out to children where the story starts and then read the book aloud.
- Invite children to retell the story by telling what happened at the beginning of the story, in the middle, and at the end.

The Monster in the Closet

Language Arts Standard: *Follows two-step requests that are sequential but not related*

- Place a stuffed toy monster inside a closet in the classroom or inside a cabinet that has a door. If a toy one is not available, a picture of a storybook monster can be used.
- Invite children to sit near the closet or cabinet that has the "monster" in it.
- Explain to them that each time the door is opened they must listen to what the monster tells them to do.
- Have children perform movements such as those listed below, with you speaking for the monster.

Jump up and down and touch your nose.
Turn around and pat your head.
Clap your hands three times and touch your knees.

Looking at Letters and Words

Language Arts Standard: *Understands that reading progresses from left to right*

- Make large letter cards that spell the word *MONSTER*.
- Write the word *MONSTER* on the board.
- Have children identify the beginning sound of the word and count the letters.
- Invite seven children to stand in front of the board and hold a letter card. Pass out the letter cards in random order.
- Challenge children who are sitting to take turns arranging those children standing in the correct order to spell the word *MONSTER*. Have children refer to the word written on the board if necessary.

Find the Monsters

Math Standard: *Uses positional terms such as in, on, over, or under*

- Duplicate and color ten monsters (p. 89). Cut them out and laminate them.

- Before class, place the monster cutouts around the room in places such as *on the shelf, under the table, behind the door, in the trash can,* or *between the chairs.*

- Invite one child at a time to find a monster and tell where it was. Depending on the class size, children may work with partners.

- Write the response on a chart, such as *Lilly's monster was on the shelf.*

- Have children follow along as all of the responses are read. Use a pointer to point to each word as it is read.

In Tune with Language

Language Arts Standard: *Recognizes and names rhyming words*

- Invite children to learn the following song to the tune of "Twinkle, Twinkle, Little Star."

There is a monster under my bed.
He has three eyes and a horn on his head.

He was afraid and needed me
To help him learn his ABCs.

Now the monster is my friend.
And I will love him 'til the end.

- Have children identify the words in the song that rhyme.

Let's Write: My Monster Friend

Language Arts Standard: *Uses scribbles, approximations of letters, or known letters to represent written language*

- Have children sing the monster song on page 85.
- Have them describe what the monster in the song looks like.
- Invite children to draw a picture of the monster including the three eyes and a horn on his head.
- Challenge them to write the ABCs on the back of the drawing for the monster. Accept scribble writing or approximations of letters from younger children.

Monster Mush

Language Arts Standard: *Engages in conversations that develop a thought or idea*

- Read a monster book from the list on page 82.
- Discuss with children what monsters might like to eat. Write their responses on a chart.
- Provide children with a small cup of flavored yogurt and a spoon.
- Fill bowls with raisins (dried ants), sunflower seeds (mice toes), and oat cereal Os (bug eyes). Put a spoon in each bowl.
- Invite children to add a spoonful of dried ants, mice toes, and bug eyes to their yogurt.

Caution: Be aware of children who may have food allergies.

Math Center

Math Standard:
Describes and extends
simple patterns

Monster Patterns

- Duplicate six monsters (p. 89). Cut them out and laminate them. The monsters can also be colored so that children can make color patterns. You may wish to enlarge some monsters so that children can make patterns such as big, little, big, little.

- Invite children to make a simple ABABAB pattern using the monsters.

- Challenge children to make other patterns with the monsters.

- Have children "read" their pattern to a friend.

Language Center

Language Arts
Standard:
Matches partner
letters

Monsters Under the Bed

- Duplicate eight monsters and eight beds (p. 90). Color them and cut them out.

- Write a target lowercase letter on the paper that each monster is holding. Laminate the monsters.

- Color the beds. Write partner letters upside down on the back of each bed. Then cut along the bedposts and fold back the bedspread to reveal the letters. Glue the beds to construction paper, leaving the bedspread flap free.

- Invite children to hide the monsters under the beds that have the correct partner letters.

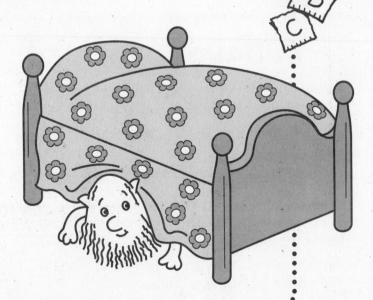

Art Center

Language Arts Standard:
Acts out plays, stories, or songs

Monster Masks

- Provide each child with a large brown grocery bag. Cut off the top one-third of each bag and cut two holes for eyes.

- Read aloud *Where the Wild Things Are* by Maurice Sendak.

- Have children name the characteristic that all of the Wild Things have in common. Guide them to say yellow eyes.

- Invite children to paint large yellow circles around the eye holes on the bag.

- Have children also paint other features such as a nose, a mouth, and eyebrows or eyelashes.

- Encourage children to use various craft items like yarn, scrap paper, buttons, pipe cleaners, and glitter to make their mask look "monstrous."

- As they listen to the story again, have children wear their mask and act like "wild things." Invite one child to pretend to be Max, if desired.

Science Center

Science Standard:
Demonstrates a willingness to take risks by choosing to participate in a variety of experiences

A Hairy Monster

- Provide children with paper cups, potting soil, a spoon, grass seeds, and markers.

- Invite them to draw a silly monster face on the side of a cup.

- Have children use the spoon to fill their cup with potting soil.

- Then have them sprinkle a generous amount of grass seeds on top of the potting soil.

- Finally, have children put a spoonful of water on the grass seeds and set the cup in the window.

- Encourage children to moisten the seeds each day and watch the monster's hair grow.

Monster Pattern

Use with "Find the Monsters" on page 85 and "Monster Patterns" on page 87.

monster

Monsters: Pattern
Sensational Seasons: Fall, SV 9781419033957

Monster and Bed Patterns

Use with "Monsters Under the Bed" on page 87.

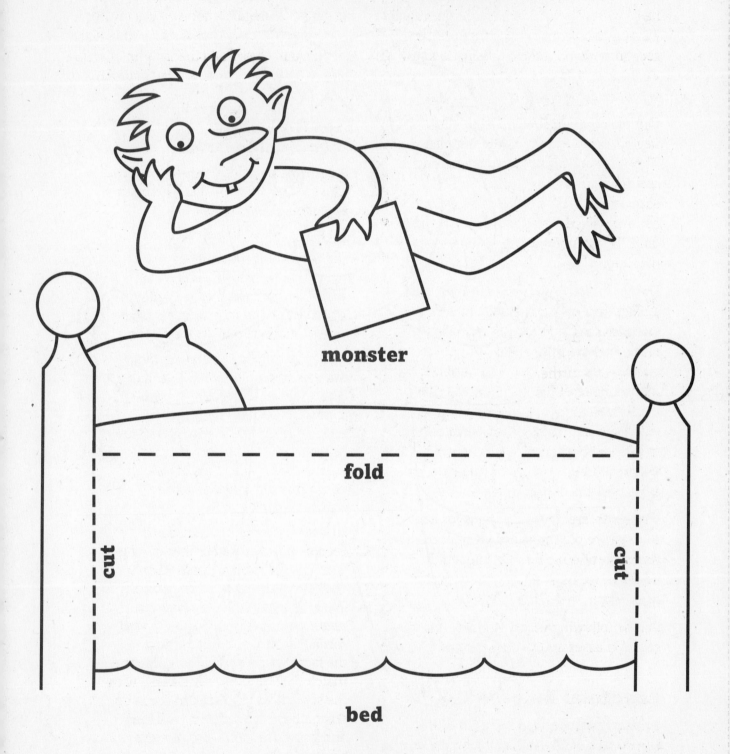

monster

fold

cut

cut

bed

Assessment

We observe children every day in our classrooms. Most of the time, these observations are done on an informal basis. We may not even realize the valuable information we gain from them. Often we recognize how much we really do know about the children in our classroom when we formally assess them.

Our observations are only the very beginning of assessment in our classrooms. The terms **assessment** and **evaluation** are often used interchangeably, yet assessment must occur before evaluation can take place. To assess means to collect data. To evaluate means to analyze that data.

During our daily observations, we collect data on each of the children in our classrooms. However, to make that assessment worthwhile, it is important to go one step further and evaluate the data that we collect. The key to assessment in our classrooms is the evaluations we make and how we use those evaluations to inform instruction. We cannot just assess children. Without evaluation, the assessment is hardly worth noting.

Just as we create lesson plans for each day, so must we plan assessment opportunities. Assessment does not just happen. In addition, we must plan time for evaluation of the data we collect.

On the following pages, you will find some valuable assessments for your preschoolers.

Anecdotal Records

An anecdotal record is a record of the behaviors a child exhibits during the day. It tells a story about what the child can do. Over time, anecdotal records create snapshots of the children in your class. Anecdotal records are probably one of the easiest assessment tools to use in your classroom. This tool is an appropriate one to use on a daily basis, and the time devoted to taking anecdotal records is very minimal.

Tips for Taking Anecdotal Records

- Keep your anecdotal record system close at hand. This will allow you to note behaviors quickly.

- Be sure to date your records.

- Set goals for the number of anecdotal records you will make each day. For instance, every day of the week you may want to make notes on one-fifth of your children.

- It may be helpful to choose a focus for your anecdotal records each day. This may be particularly helpful if you are just beginning to use anecdotal records in your classroom. For example, one week you may want to note what kinds of writing each child is engaged in during writing activities.

- Attempt to keep your anecdotal records positive. Rather than noting what a child **can't** do, note what he or she **can** do instead. For example, *Today Mary was able to navigate a return sweep while reading her guided reading book.* Don't worry about the fact that the child wasn't able to match the written words entirely with the spoken words. Keep the focus on what children can do. You will then find your instruction also remains positive.

- Set aside time at least once a month to review and evaluate your anecdotal records. Note any patterns you find within a group of students or a pattern you see emerging with one particular child.

- Use your anecdotal records to inform your instruction. For instance, if you find a group of children who are continually attempting to write poetry during writing time, you may want to pull them together to talk about various types of poetry writing. If you note a group of children who are having difficulty retelling stories they have read, pull them together in a group to work on retelling simple stories. These examples illustrate the use of anecdotal records to inform your instruction.

Organizing Anecdotal Records

The following is just one organizational system that can help to make your use of anecdotal records efficient. Write each child's name at the bottom of a 4″ x 6″ ruled index card. Then lay the index cards on a clipboard in a layered effect. Attach the cards with tape.

As you plan your assessment opportunities, keep the clipboard and a pen—which can be attached to the clipboard with a string—with you. Note behaviors you observe on a child's index card. Be sure to date your observations. Plan to note behaviors for at least one-fifth of the children in your class each day. That will allow you to have at least one anecdotal record for each child each week.

As you fill index cards, replace them. File the completed cards in your children's portfolios.

Anecdotal records can be taken for any subject. Be sure not only to date your anecdotal records, but to record the subject matter so you can quickly look through the records and find patterns in a particular subject. Once a month, spend five to ten minutes rereading the anecdotal records on one child. Look for patterns to address in your instruction.

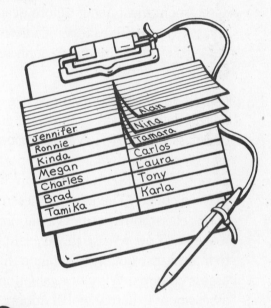

ABC/Phonemic Awareness Assessment

To assess children's alphabet knowledge, copy the ABC assessment card on page 94. Laminate it for durability. Also make copies of the ABC assessment recording sheet on this page. Plan to assess children on their alphabet knowledge a minimum of twice a year, once at the beginning and once at the end.

Teacher Directions:

- As you call a child over to work with you, show him or her the ABC assessment card. Say to the child: **What are these?** Do not use the word "letters," as you will want to note what the child calls these symbols.
- Show only one row of letters at a time. This will allow children to focus better.
- Point to each letter and say: **Tell me what this is.** The child should tell you the name of the letter. Record the child's response.
- You can also use these blackline masters to assess phonemic awareness. Simply point to each letter and say: **Tell me what sound this letter makes.**

Child's Name: _____ Date: _____

Child's Approximate Age: _____ Child's Score: _____ /54

Ask: **What are these?** Child's response: _____

✔ = correct response   x = incorrect response   O = no response

a ___	e ___	i ___	m ___	q ___	u ___	y ___
b ___	f ___	j ___	n ___	r ___	v ___	z ___
c ___	g ___	k ___	o ___	s ___	w ___	a ___
d ___	h ___	l ___	p ___	t ___	x ___	g ___
A ___	E ___	I ___	M ___	Q ___	U ___	Y ___
B ___	F ___	J ___	N ___	R ___	V ___	Z ___
C ___	G ___	K ___	O ___	S ___	W ___	
D ___	H ___	L ___	P ___	T ___	X ___	

Assessment
Sensational Seasons: Fall, SV 9781419033957

ABC Assessment Card

a   e   i   m   q   u   y

b   f   j   n   r   v   z

c   g   k   o   s   w   a

d   h   l   p   t   x   g

. . . .

A   E   I   M   Q   U   Y

B   F   J   N   R   V   Z

C   G   K   O   S   W

D   H   L   P   T   X

Assessment
Sensational Seasons: Fall, SV 9781419033957

Emergent Reading Checklist

Teacher Directions:

During whole-group, small-group, or independent reading time, observe children as they are engaged in the reading process. Be sure to note a child's reading behavior at least once each quarter during the year. This checklist can also be useful at report card time.

Name: _____ Grade: _____

	Date of Entries ✔			
Enjoys listening to books				
Confidently participates in shared reading				
Makes meaningful predictions using the story and pictures as clues				
Retells stories and rhymes				
Approximates book language				
Uses pictures to comprehend text				
Realizes that print carries a message				
Demonstrates book handling skills				
Locates the name of the author and illustrator				
Recognizes parts of a book (cover, title, title page)				
Demonstrates directionality: left to right				
Demonstrates directionality: top to bottom				
Identifies uppercase and lowercase letters				
Demonstrates an understanding of letters and words				
Identifies some sounds				
Matches spoken words to print				
Recognizes own name and common environmental print				
Reads some one-syllable and high-frequency words				
Chooses to look at/read books from a variety of sources				
Can sit still for short periods of time to read a book				

Checklist
Sensational Seasons: Fall, SV 9781419033957

Emergent Writing Checklist

Teacher Directions:

Observe children during whole-group writing experiences and independent writing experiences. Be sure to note student writing behavior at least once each quarter during the year. This checklist can also be useful at report card time.

Name: _____ Grade: _____

	Date of Entries			✔
Makes pre-letter writing marks on paper				
Writes letters, symbols, or numerals randomly				
Writes some uppercase and lowercase letters of the alphabet				
Demonstrates directionality of letters				
Writes initial consonants				
Writes partially phonetically spelled words				
Writes some completely phonetically spelled words				
Writes high-frequency words randomly				
Writes a few known words correctly				
Uses random finger pointing when reading his or her writing				

Checklist
Sensational Seasons: Fall, SV 9781419033957